ARKANSAS BAIL BOND LAWS AND REGULATIONS

Second Edition, 2010-2011

Law Offices of Lisa Douglas, PLLC
2300 Main Street
North Little Rock, AR 72114
501-798-0004
www.LisaGDouglas.com
LisaGDouglas@aol.com

- and -

John Wesley Hall
1311 Broadway Street
Little Rock, Arkansas 72202
501-371-9131
www.JohnWesleyHall.com
ForHall@aol.com
Best Lawyers in America, Criminal Defense
Past President, National Association of Criminal Defense Lawyers

NOTICE

This book is complete through June 2010. When the General Assembly meets January to April 2011, there likely will be changes.

Also, the Bail Bond Board could amend its regulations anytime. If so, this book will be republished.

TABLE OF CONTENTS

Part I. Arkansas Statutes. 1

Part II. Summary of Case Law on Right to Pursue a Fugitive. 55

Part III. Rules and Regulations of the Arkansas Bail Bond Board. 63

Part IV. IRS Form 8300, Reporting Cash Transactions over $10,000. 111

PART I. ARKANSAS STATUTES

Criminal Offenses, Title 5

Chapter 39 Burglary, Trespass, and Other Intrusions

§ 5-39-201   Residential burglary – Commercial burglary. 1
§ 5-39-202   Breaking or entering.. 2
§ 5-39-203   Criminal trespass. 2
§ 5-39-204   Aggravated residential burglary. 2

Chapter 54.   Obstructing Governmental Operations

§ 5-54-120   Failure to Appear. 3

Chapter 71.   Riots, Disorderly Conduct

§ 5-71-208   Harassment.. 4
§ 5-71-229   Stalking.. 5

Local Government, Title 14

Chapter 52.   Municipal Police Departments

§ 14-52-112 Fees for bail or delivery bond 7

Practice, Procedure and Courts, Title 16

Chapter 19.   Justice of the Peace Courts

§ 16-19-408 Improper Venue of Action. 7

Chapter 81.   Arrest

§ 16-81-109 Bail. 8
§ 16-81-110 Return on Warrant. 8

Chapter 84.   Bail Generally

§ 16-84-101 Definitions. 9
§ 16-84-102 Persons Authorized to Take Bail. 9
§ 16-84-103 Qualification of Surety. 10
§ 16-84-104 Additional Security. 10
§ 16-84-105 Responsibility of Officer Taking Bail. 11
§ 16-84-106 Attorneys and Officers Not to Be Sureties. 11
§ 16-84-107 Form of Bond. 12
§ 16-84-108 Bonds not Void For Want of Form. 12
§ 16-84-109 Irregularity of Bail Bond or Recognizance. 13
§ 16-84-110 Bail Before Conviction. 13
§ 16-84-111 Bail During Trial. 13
§ 16-84-112 Entering of Recognizance on Court Minutes. 14
§ 16-84-113 Application for Bail. 14
§ 16-84-114 Surrender of Defendant. 14
§ 16-84-115 Deposit of Money in Lieu of Bail. 15
§ 16-84-116 Recommitment after Bail or Deposit of Money. 16
§ 16-84-201 Action on Bonds in District Courts. 17
§ 16-84-202 Disposition of Deposit. 18
§ 16-84-203 Certain Absences Excused. 18
§ 16-84-207 Action on Bonds in Circuit Courts. 19

Chapter 85.   Pretrial Proceedings

§ 16-85-101 Right to Attorney, Physician, and Phone Calls. 21

Chapter 90.   Judgment and Sentence Generally

    § 16-90-105 Verdict of Guilty 22

Chapter 94.   Extradition

    § 16-94-216 Bail. 23
    § 16-94-217 Discharge of Warrant. 23

Professions, Occupations and Business, Title 17

Chapter 19.   Bail Bondsmen

    § 17-19-101 Definitions. 24
    § 17-19-102 Penalties.. 24
    § 17-19-103 Civil and Criminal Proceedings. 24
    § 17-19-104 Exemption. 25
    § 17-19-105 Prohibitions. 25
    § 17-19-106 Bail Bond Company and Licensing Board. 25
    § 17-19-107 Exception to Education Requirements. 26
    § 17-19-108 Rules and Regulations. 26
    § 17-19-109 Advertising. 27
    § 17-19-110 Licensed Bail Bond Agent. 27
    § 17-19-111 Fees.. 28
    § 17-19-201 Licenses Required. 30
    § 17-19-202 Applications. 31
    § 17-19-203 Character References. 33
    § 17-19-204 Examination. 34
    § 17-19-205 Letter of Credit or Certificate of Deposit Required. 35
    § 17-19-206 Duties of Board and Clerks 35
    § 17-19-207 Expiration and Renewal. 36
    § 17-19-208 Civil Action Administrative Action 37
    § 17-19-209 Violations/Hearings 38
    § 17-19-210 Suspension/Review. 40
    § 17-19-211 Administrative Penalty. 41
    § 17-19-212 Licenses. 41
    § 17-19-301 Premiums.. 42
    § 17-19-302 Collateral – Receipt Required. 45
    § 17-19-303 Bail Bonds – Numbers – Report.. 45
    § 17-19-304 Maximum Amount of Unsecured Bond. 46

§ 17-19-305 Appearance Bond............................... 46
§ 17-19-306 Posting of Bondsmen List. 46
§ 17-19-401 Requirements................................. 48
§ 17-19-402 Establishment of Program Schedule of Fees.......... 49

Arkansas Court Rules

Arkansas Rules of Appellate Procedure—Criminal

Rule 6. Bail on appeal.. 50

Arkansas Rules of Criminal Procedure

Rule 9.1. Release on Order to Appear or on Defendant's own Recognizance. 51
Rule 9.2. Release on Money Bail............................... 52
Rule 9.3. Prohibition of Wrongful Acts Pending Trial................. 53

PART II. SUMMARY OF CASE LAW
ON RIGHT TO PURSUE A FUGITIVE

State v. Mathis, 349 N.C. 503, 509 S.E. 2d 155 (1998)...................... 55

Other cases... 61

PART III. RULES AND REGULATIONS
OF THE ARKANSAS BAIL BOND BOARD

Rule and Regulation 1, Regulation of Bail Bond Business...................... 63

1.   Purpose................................... 68
2.   Authority.................................. 68
3.   Effective Date and Applicability.................... 69
4.   Definitions................................. 69
5.   Bail Bond Form.............................. 70
6.   Qualifying Power of Attorney Form. 70
7.   Regular Power of Attorney Form..................... 71
8.   Company Codes.............................. 72
9.   Quarterly Reports............................. 72

10.	Secured Bail Bonds.	73
11.	Unsecured Bond Commitment; Penalties.	73
12.	Clean Irrevocable Letter of Credit.	74
13.	Certificate of Deposit.	74
14.	Certificate of Deposit and Clean Irrevocable Letter of Credit; Release.	75
15.	Licenses.	75
16.	License Required.	76
17.	Transfer of Bondsman License.	77
18.	License Renewal, Continuing Education Required.	79
19.	License Denial – Company.	80
20.	License Denial – Bondsman.	80
21.	Financial Statements; Guidelines	81
22.	Collateral; Fiduciary Relationship.	82
23.	Return of Excess Collateral on Forfeiture; Expenses.	82
24.	Refund of Premium.	83
25.	Allowable Charges.	83
26.	Forfeitures; Misrepresentations.	84
27.	Unpaid Forfeitures and Misconduct; License Sanctions.	84
28.	Bail Bond Complaint Form and Procedures.	85
29.	Complaints, Cooperation Required.	85
30.	Hearing Officer.	86
31.	Hearings, Revocation or Suspension of License.	86
32.	Gifts Prohibited.	88
33.	Notice of Change of Address.	88
34.	Written Statement of Bail Transaction; Contents.	88
35.	Examinations.	89
36.	Record Retention.	89
37.	Company Appointment.	89
38.	Advertising.	90
39.	Apprehension of Defendants.	90
40.	Compliance with Posted Rules of Jails.	91
41.	Severability.	91

Appendix A – Bail Bond Form.	93
Appendix B – Affidavit of Sole Proprietorship.	94
Appendix C – Statement of Bail and Payment Received.	95
Appendix D – Qualifying Power of Attorney.	96
Appendix E – Quarterly Report Form.	97
Appendix F – Clean Irrevocable Letter of Credit.	99
Appendix G – Bail Bond Complaint Form.	102
Appendix H – Advertising Examples.	104

Appendix I – Authorization by Surety to Arrest Defendant on Bail Bond. . . 105
Appendix J – Collateral Receipt (Example). 106

Rule and Regulation 2, Regulation of the Education Program. 107

    1.   Purpose 107
    2.   Authority 107
    3.   Effective Date and Applicability 107
    4.   Definitions 108
    5.   Application for Course Approval 109
    6.   Approval or Denial of Course 109
    7.   Approval of Fee for Continuing Education Course 109
    8.   Certificate of Completion 110
    9.   Severability. 110

PART IV. IRS FORM 8300
REPORTING CASH TRANSACTIONS OVER $10,000

26 U.S.C. § 6050I. 113
    Authors' Endnotes to § 6050I. 116
IRS's Frequently Asked Questions. 119
IRS Form 8300 (http://www.irs.gov/pub/irs-pdf/f8300.pdf)
    www.irs.gov; search for "8300". 126

Criminal Offenses, Title 5

Chapter 39. Burglary, Trespass, and Other Intrusions[1]

§ 5-39-201. Residential burglary – Commercial burglary

(a)(1) A person commits residential burglary if he or she enters or remains unlawfully in a residential occupiable structure of another person with the purpose of committing in the residential occupiable structure any offense punishable by imprisonment.

    (2)   Residential burglary is a Class B felony.

(b)(1) A person commits commercial burglary if he or she enters or remains unlawfully in a commercial occupiable structure of another person with the purpose of committing in the commercial occupiable structure any offense punishable by imprisonment.

    (2)   Commercial burglary is a Class C felony.

History: Acts 1975, No. 280, § 2002; A.S.A. 1947, § 41-2002; Acts 1993, No. 442, § 2; 1993, No. 552, § 2.

§ 5-39-202. Breaking or entering

(a)   A person commits the offense of breaking or entering if for the purpose of committing a theft or felony he or she breaks or enters into any:

(1)   Building, structure, or vehicle;
(2)   Vault, safe, cash register, safety deposit box, or money depository;
(3)   Money vending machine, coin-operated amusement machine, vending machine, or product dispenser;
(4)   Coin telephone or coin box;
(5)   Fare box on a bus; or
(6)   Other similar container, apparatus, or equipment.

(b)   [Each such entry as in (a) is a separate offense.]

---

[1] Note: See Part II on the Summary of Case Law on the Right to Pursue a Fugitive.

(c)   Breaking or entering is a Class D felony.

History: Acts 1975, No. 280, § 2003; A.S.A. 1947, § 41-2003; Acts 1993, No. 296, § 1.

§ 5-39-203. Criminal trespass

(a)   A person commits criminal trespass if he or she purposely enters or remains unlawfully in or upon:
(1)   A vehicle; or
(2)   The premises of another person.
(b)   Criminal trespass is a:
(1)   Class B misdemeanor if the vehicle or premises involved is an occupiable structure; or
(2)   Class C misdemeanor if otherwise committed.

History: Acts 1975, No. 280, § 2004; A.S.A. 1947, § 41-2004

§ 5-39-204. Aggravated residential burglary

(a)   A person commits aggravated residential burglary if he or she commits residential burglary as defined in § 5-39-201 of a residential occupiable structure occupied by any person, and he or she:
(1)   Is armed with a deadly weapon or represents by word or conduct that he or she is armed with a deadly weapon; or
(2)   Inflicts or attempts to inflict death or serious physical injury upon another person.

(b)   Aggravated residential burglary is a Class Y felony.

History: Acts 2007, No. 1608, § 1.

Chapter 54. Obstructing Governmental Operations

§ 5-54-120. Failure to appear

(a)   A person commits the offense of failure to appear if he or she fails to appear without reasonable excuse subsequent to having been:

(1)   Cited or summonsed as an accused; or

(2)   Lawfully set at liberty upon condition that he or she appear at a specified time, place, and court.

(b)   Failure to appear is a Class C felony if the required appearance was to answer a charge of felony or for disposition of any felony charge either before or after a determination of guilt of the felony charge.

(c)(1) Failure to appear is a Class A misdemeanor if the required appearance was to answer a charge of misdemeanor or for disposition of any misdemeanor charge either before or after a determination of guilt of the misdemeanor charge.

(2)   Failure to appear is a Class C misdemeanor if the required appearance was to answer a violation.

(d)   This section does not apply to an order to appear imposed as a condition of suspension or probation pursuant to § 5-4-303 or an order to appear issued prior to a revocation hearing pursuant to § 5-4-310.

History: Acts 1975, No. 280, § 2820; A.S.A. 1947, § 41-2820; Acts 1991, No. 916, § 1.

Chapter 71. Riots, Disorderly Conduct, Etc.

§ 5-71-208. Harassment

(a)   A person commits the offense of harassment if, with purpose to harass, annoy, or alarm another person, without good cause, he or she:

(1)   Strikes, shoves, kicks, or otherwise touches a person, subjects that person to offensive physical contact or attempts or threatens to do so;

(2)   In a public place, directs obscene language or makes an obscene gesture to or at another person in a manner likely to provoke a violent or disorderly response;

(3)   Follows a person in or about a public place;

(4)   In a public place repeatedly insults, taunts, or challenges another person in a manner likely to provoke a violent or disorderly response;

(5)   Engages in conduct or repeatedly commits an act that alarms or seriously annoys another person and that serves no legitimate purpose; or

(6)   Places a person under surveillance by remaining present outside that person's school, place of employment, vehicle, other place occupied by that person, or residence, other than the residence of the defendant, for no purpose other than to harass, alarm, or annoy.

(b)   Harassment is a Class A misdemeanor.

(c)   It is an affirmative defense to prosecution under this section if the actor is a law enforcement officer, licensed private investigator, attorney, process server, licensed bail bondsman, or a store detective acting within the reasonable scope of his or her duty while conducting surveillance on an official work assignment.

(d)(1)   Upon pretrial release of the defendant, a judicial officer shall enter a no contact order in writing consistent with Rules 9.3 and 9.4 of the Arkansas Rules of Criminal Procedure and shall give notice to the defendant of penalties contained in Rule 9.5 of the Arkansas Rules of Criminal Procedure.
(2)   This no contact order remains in effect during the pendency of any appeal of a conviction under this section.
(3)   The judicial officer or prosecuting attorney shall provide a copy of this no contact order to the victim and arresting agency without unnecessary delay.

(e)   If the judicial officer has reason to believe that mental disease or defect of the defendant will or has become an issue in the cause, the judicial officer shall enter such orders as are consistent with § 5-2-305.

History: Acts 1975, No. 280, § 2909; 1985, No. 711, § 1; A.S.A. 1947, § 41-2909; Acts 1993, No. 379, § 5; 1993, No. 388, § 5; 1995, No. 1302, § 3.

§ 5-71-229. Stalking

(a)(1)   A person commits stalking in the first degree if he or she purposely engages in a course of conduct that harasses another person and makes a terroristic threat with the intent of placing that person in imminent fear of death or serious bodily injury or placing that person in imminent fear of the death or serious bodily injury of his or her immediate family and the person:
(A)   Does so in contravention of an order of protection consistent with The Domestic Abuse Act of 1991, § 9-15-101 et seq., or a no contact order as set out in subdivision (a)(2)(A) of this section, protecting the same victim, or any other order issued by any court protecting the same victim;
(B)   Has been convicted within the previous ten (10) years of:

(i)   Stalking in the second degree;

(ii)   Violating § 5-13-301 or § 5-13-310; or

(iii)   Stalking or threats against another person's safety under the statutory provisions of any other state jurisdiction; or

(C)   Is armed with a deadly weapon or represents by word or conduct that he or she is armed with a deadly weapon.

(2)(A) Upon pretrial release of the defendant, a judicial officer shall enter a no contact order in writing consistent with Rules 9.3 and 9.4 of the Arkansas Rules of Criminal Procedure and shall give notice to the defendant of penalties contained in Rule 9.5 of the Arkansas Rules of Criminal Procedure.

(B)   This no contact order remains in effect during the pendency of any appeal of a conviction under subsection (a) of this section.

(C)   The judicial officer or prosecuting attorney shall provide a copy of this no contact order to the victim and the arresting agency without unnecessary delay.

(D)   If the judicial officer has reason to believe that mental disease or defect of the defendant will or has become an issue in the cause, the judicial officer shall enter such orders as are consistent with § 5-2-305.

(3) Stalking in the first degree is a Class B felony.

(b)(1) A person commits stalking in the second degree if he or she purposely engages in a course of conduct that harasses another person and makes a terroristic threat with the intent of placing that person in imminent fear of death or serious bodily injury or placing that person in imminent fear of the death or serious bodily injury of his or her immediate family.

(2)(A) Upon pretrial release of the defendant, a judicial officer shall enter a no contact order in writing consistent with Rules 9.3 and 9.4 of the Arkansas Rules of Criminal Procedure and shall give notice to the defendant of penalties contained in Rule 9.5 of the Arkansas Rules of Criminal Procedure.

(B)   This no contact order remains in effect during the pendency of any appeal of a conviction under subsection (b) of this section.

(C)   The judicial officer or prosecuting attorney shall provide a copy of this no contact order to the victim and arresting agency without unnecessary delay.

(D)   If the judicial officer has reason to believe that mental disease or defect of the defendant will or has become an issue in the cause, the judicial officer shall enter such orders as are consistent with § 5-2-305.

(3)   Stalking in the second degree is a Class C felony.

(c)   It is an affirmative defense to prosecution under this section if the actor is a law enforcement officer, licensed private investigator, attorney, process server, licensed bail bondsman, or a store detective acting within the reasonable scope of his or her duty while conducting surveillance on an official work assignment.

(d)   As used in this section:

(1)(A) "Course of conduct" means a pattern of conduct composed of two (2) or more acts separated by at least thirty-six (36) hours, but occurring within one (1) year.

(B)(i) "Course of conduct" does not include constitutionally protected activity.

(ii) If the defendant claims that he or she was engaged in a constitutionally protected activity, the court shall determine the validity of that claim as a matter of law and, if found valid, shall exclude that activity from evidence;

(2)   "Harasses" means an act of harassment as prohibited by § 5-71-208; and

(3)   "Immediate family" means any spouse, parent, child, any person related by consanguinity or affinity within the second degree, or any other person who regularly resides in the household or who, within the prior six (6) months, regularly resided in the household.

History: Acts 1993, No. 379, §§ 1-3; 1993, No. 388, §§ 1-3; 1995, No. 1302, § 1; 2007, No. 827, § 94.

Local Government, Title 14

Chapter 52. Municipal Police Departments

§ 14-52-111. Fees for bail or delivery bond

Every municipal police department in this state is authorized to charge and collect a twenty dollar ($20.00) fee for taking and entering every bail or delivery bond.

History: Acts 1997, No. 252, § 1; 2003, No. 1347, § 1.

Practice, Procedure and Courts, Title 16

Chapter 19. Justice Of The Peace Courts

§ 16-19-408. Improper venue of action

(a)   Whenever an objection is made by a defendant in any action cognizable before a justice of the peace or a municipal court, instituted by summons or warrant, or in an action by an attachment, an action for the recovery of personal property, an action by provisional remedy, or in any criminal action or proceeding, that the action was brought before a justice of the peace or a municipal court wherein the venue is improper under the laws of the State of Arkansas, the court shall immediately hear proof on the question. If it is established by proof that the venue is improper, then all further proceedings shall be discontinued and the justice of the peace or clerk of the municipal court shall transmit to a justice of the peace or municipal court wherein the venue is proper all the original papers in the case, including the bail bond, if there is any.

(b)   If the defendant is in custody, he shall be taken and delivered before the justice of the peace or the municipal court, and the bail, if any, shall be liable for the appearance of the defendant in the court to which the papers are transmitted.

(c)   The court to which the papers are transmitted shall proceed to try the action in all respects as if the action had been originally brought to the court.

History: Acts 1949, No. 224, § 1; A.S.A. 1947, § 26-310.

Chapter 81. Arrest

§ 16-81-109. Bail

(a)(1) When any sheriff or other law enforcement officer makes an arrest, he or she is authorized to take and to approve bail in the manner provided by law wherever he or she makes the arrest.

(2) If the offense charged is a misdemeanor, the person arrested may immediately give bail for appearing on a day to be named in the bail bond before the judge or magistrate who issued the warrant or before the court having jurisdiction to try the offense. The sheriff or other officer making the arrest may be authorized by the judge or magistrate issuing the warrant to take the bail by an endorsement made on the warrant to that effect.

(b)(1) If the defendant gives bail for his or her appearance before the judge or magistrate for an examination of the charge, as provided in subsection (a) of this section, the sheriff or officer taking the bail shall fix the day of the defendant's appearance.

(2) A deviation from the provisions of subdivision (b)(1) of this section shall not, however, render the bail bond invalid.

History: Crim. Code, §§ 25-27; Acts 1871, No. 49, § 1 [25]; C. & M. Dig., §§ 2896-2898; Init. Meas. 1936, No. 3, § 19, Acts 1937, p. 1384; Pope's Dig., §§ 3712-3714, 3865; A.S.A. 1947, §§ 43-411, 43-418–43-420; Acts 2005, No. 1994, § 268.

§ 16-81-110. Return on the warrant

(a)(1) The sheriff or officer who has executed a warrant of arrest shall make a written return on the warrant of the time and manner of executing it and deliver the warrant to the judge or magistrate before whom the defendant is brought.

(2) If bail is given as provided in § 16-81-109(a)(2), the officer shall deliver the warrant and bail bond to the judge or magistrate before whom, or to the clerk of the court in which, the defendant is bound by the bail bond to appear.

(b) If the arrest is made in a different county from that in which the offense is charged to have been committed and bail is given, the sheriff or officer may transmit the warrant and bail bond by mail to the person to whom by subsection (a) of this section he or she is required to deliver them.

History: Crim. Code, §§ 30, 31; C. & M. Dig., §§ 2901, 2902; Pope's Dig., §§ 3717, 3718; A.S.A. 1947, §§ 43-421, 43-422; Acts 2005, No. 1994, § 268.

Chapter 84. Bail Generally

§ 16-84-101. Definitions

As used in this chapter:

(1) "Admission to bail" means an order from a competent court or magistrate that the defendant be discharged from actual custody on bail and fixing the amount of the bail;

(2) "Direct supervision" means the person is in the physical presence of and acting pursuant to instructions from an Arkansas-licensed bail bond agent;

(3) "Professional bail bondsman" means an individual licensed as a professional bail bondsman by the Professional Bail Bond Company and Professional Bail Bondsman Licensing Board pursuant to § 17-19-201 et seq.;

(4) "Professional bail bond company" means a person holding a professional bail bond company license issued by the Professional Bail Bond Company and Professional Bail Bondsman Licensing Board pursuant to § 17-19-201 et seq.;

(5) "Surety" means the person who becomes the surety for the appearance of the defendant in court; and

(6)(A) "Taking of bail" or "take bail" means the acceptance by a person authorized to take bail of the undertaking of a sufficient surety for the appearance of the defendant according to the terms of the undertaking, or that the surety will pay to the court the sum specified.

(B) "Taking of bail" or "take bail" shall not include the fixing of the amount of bail and no person other than a competent court or magistrate shall fix the amount of bail.

History: Acts 1989, No. 417, § 5; 1997, No. 973, § 1; 2001, No. 1387, § 1.

§ 16-84-102. Persons authorized to take bail

(a) The following may take bail:

(1) A judge, magistrate, or clerk of the court;

(2) A sheriff or deputy sheriff with respect to any person committed to the common jail of the county;

(3) Any law enforcement officer designated by a municipal police department with respect to any person committed to a municipal jail; and

(4) A law enforcement officer making an arrest as authorized under § 16-81-109.

(b) A constable shall not take bail.

History: Acts 1989, No. 417, § 5; 2005, No. 1994, § 270.

§ 16-84-103. Qualification of surety

(a) The surety shall be:

(1) A professional bail bondsman acting through a professional bail bond company; or

(2) A resident of the state, owner of visible property, over and above that exempt from execution, to the value of the sum in which bail is required, and shall be worth that amount after the payment of the surety's debts and liabilities.

(b)(1)(A)(i) The person or persons offered as surety shall be examined on oath in regard to qualifications as surety, and any officer authorized to take bail is authorized to administer the oath, reduce the statements on oath to writing, and require the person or persons offered as surety to sign the statement.

(ii) Other proof may also be taken in regard to the sufficiency of the surety.

(B) Prior to submission to the court or magistrate, the statement shall also be signed by the sheriff or chief of police in the jurisdiction where the defendant is charged.

(2) Proof that the surety is a licensed professional bail bondsman shall be deemed sufficient proof of the sufficiency of the surety, and the surety shall be accepted by all courts in this state or by any individual authorized to take bail under the provisions of § 16-84-102.

(c) No person shall be taken as surety unless the court or magistrate is satisfied, from proof and examination on oath, of the sufficiency of the person according to the requisitions of subsection (b) of this section.

(d) Where more than one (1) person is offered as surety, they shall be deemed sufficient if, in the aggregate, they possess the qualifications required.

History: Acts 1989, No. 417, § 5; 1997, No. 973, § 2; 2003, No. 1648, § 1.

§ 16-84-104. Additional security

There shall be no rules, regulations, or requirements enacted by any judge, magistrate, sheriff, or other officer of the court, requiring any professional bail bondsman or professional bail bond company to post any sum of security in addition to that required by the Professional Bail Bond Company and Professional Bail Bondsman Licensing Board pursuant to § 17-19-205 as a requirement for acceptance or writing bail bonds.

History: Acts 1989, No. 417, § 5; 1997, No. 973, § 3.

§ 16-84-105. Responsibility of officer taking bail

(a)   The officer who takes bail shall be officially responsible for the sufficiency of the surety if taken other than through a professional bail bondsman.

(b)   If the surety is not a professional bail bondsman, and the defendant has not yet appeared before a judicial officer pursuant to Rule 9 of the Arkansas Rules of Criminal Procedure, the officer shall file a statement with the court describing the property of the surety upon which the sufficiency of the surety is based. The description of the property shall include the value of the property. The statement shall also be signed by the sheriff or chief of police in the jurisdiction where the defendant is charged.

(c)   The officer who takes bail shall give a prenumbered written receipt for the collateral. The receipt shall give in detail a full account of the collateral received.

(d)   An officer who takes bail shall not be liable for any bond ordered by a judicial officer under Rule 9.2(b)(i) or (ii) of the Arkansas Rules of Criminal Procedure.

History: Acts 1989, No. 417, § 5; 1995, No. 470, § 1.

§ 16-84-106. Attorneys and officers not to be sureties

No attorney, solicitor, or counselor at law or in equity, clerk, sheriff, chief of police, law enforcement officer, or other person concerned in the execution of any process, shall become a personal guarantor or surety in any criminal proceeding.

History: Acts 1989, No. 417, § 5; 1997, No. 1046, § 1.

§ 16-84-107. Form of bond

(a) The undertaking of the surety, other than by a professional bail bondsman, shall be substantially as follows:

"A.B., being in custody, charged with the offense of (naming or briefly describing it), and being admitted to bail in the sum of dollars, we C.D., of (stating his place of residence), and E.F., of (stating his place of residence), hereby undertake that the above named A.B. shall appear in the court on the day of its term to answer said charge, and shall at all times render himself or herself amenable to the orders and process of said court in prosecution of said charge, and, if convicted, shall render himself in execution thereof; or if he fail to perform either of these conditions, that we will pay to the appropriate court the sum of dollars."

(b) If the surety is a professional bail bondsman, the undertaking of the surety shall be in a form prescribed by the regulations of the Professional Bail Bond Company and Professional Bail Bondsman Licensing Board.

History: Acts 1989, No. 417, § 5; 1997, No. 973, § 4.

§ 16-84-108. Bonds not void for want of form

No prosecution, appeal, nonresident, or attachment bond, nor any other statutory bonds of any party, plaintiff, or defendant in any court of justice, in this state, nor any recognizance in any criminal cause in this state, shall be declared null and void for the want of form if the intent of the bond can be plainly deduced from the body of the bond or recognizance.

History: Acts 1989, No. 417, § 5.1.

§ 16-84-109. Irregularity of bail bond or recognizance

(a) No bail bond or recognizance shall be deemed to be invalid by:

(1) Reason of any variance between its stipulations and the provisions of this chapter;

(2) The failure of the judge or magistrate or officer to transmit or deliver the bail bond or recognizance at the times provided in this subchapter; or

(3) Any other irregularity so that it is made to appear that the defendant was:

(A) Legally in custody;

(B)(i) Charged with the public offense; and

(ii) Discharged from the offense by reason of the giving of the bond or recognizance; and

(C) Can be ascertained from the bond or recognizance, that the surety undertook that the defendant should appear before a judge or magistrate for the trial of the offense.

(b)(1) If no day is fixed for the appearance, or an impossible day, or a day in vacation, the bond or recognizance, if for his or her appearance before a judge or magistrate, shall be considered as binding the defendant so to appear and surrender himself or herself into custody for an examination of the charge in twenty (20) days from the time of his or her giving the bond or recognizance.

(2) The bond or recognizance, if for his or her appearance for trial in court, shall be considered as binding the defendant to appear and surrender himself or herself into custody on the first day of the next term of the court which shall commence more than ten (10) days after the giving of the bond or recognizance.

History: Acts 1989, No. 417, § 5; 2005, No. 1994, § 271.

§ 16-84-110. Bail before conviction

Before conviction, the defendant may be admitted to bail for his or her appearance:

(1) Before a judge or magistrate for an examination of the charge, where the offense charged is a misdemeanor;

(2) In the court to which he or she is sent for trial;

(3) To answer an indictment which has been found against him or her; or

(4) In a criminal action.

History: Acts 1989, No. 417, § 5; 2005, No. 1994, § 271.

§ 16-84-111. Bail during trial

(a) During the trial of an indictment for a misdemeanor, the defendant may remain on bail.

(b) However, for a felony when a defendant is upon bail, he or she may remain upon bail or be kept in actual custody as the court may direct. If the defendant remains on bail, any surety's liability shall be exonerated unless the surety has agreed to remain as the surety until final judgment is rendered.

History: Acts 1989, No. 417, § 5.

§ 16-84-112. Entering of recognizance on court minutes

All recognizances required or authorized to be taken in any criminal proceeding, in open court, by any court of record shall be entered on the minutes of the court, and the substance thereof shall be read to the person recognized.

History: Acts 1989, No. 417, § 5.

§ 16-84-113. Application for bail

(a)   If the defendant is committed to jail and the application for bail is made to a judge or magistrate during vacation, it must be by written petition signed by the defendant or his or her counsel briefly stating the offense for which he or she is committed and naming the persons offered as surety.

(b)   In all other cases, the application may be made orally to the judge or magistrate.

History: Acts 1989, No. 417, § 5; 2005, No. 1994, § 272.

§ 16-84-114. Surrender of defendant

(a)(1) At any time before the forfeiture of their bond, the surety may surrender the defendant or the defendant may surrender himself or herself to the jailer of the county in which the offense was committed.

(2)   However, the surrender must be accompanied by a certified copy of the bail bond to be delivered to the jailer, who must detain the defendant in custody thereon as upon a commitment and give a written acknowledgment of the surrender.

(3)   The surety shall thereupon be exonerated.

(b)(1) For the purpose of surrendering the defendant, the surety may obtain from the officer having in his or her custody the bail bond or recognizance a certified copy thereof, and thereupon at any place in the state may arrest the defendant.

(2)   No person other than an Arkansas-licensed bail bond agent, an Arkansas-licensed private investigator, a certified law enforcement officer, or a person acting under the direct supervision of an Arkansas-licensed bail bond agent shall be authorized to apprehend, detain, or arrest a defendant on a bail bond, wherever issued, unless that person is licensed as a bail bond agent by the state where the bail bond was written.

(3)   No person shall represent himself or herself to be a bail enforcement agent, bounty hunter, or similar title in this state.

(4)   Any bail bond agent attempting to apprehend a defendant shall notify the local law enforcement agency or agencies of his or her presence and provide the local law enforcement agency or agencies with the defendant's name, charges, and suspected location.

(5)   Any person who violates any provision of this section shall be guilty of a Class D felony.

(c)   The surety may arrest the defendant without the certified copy.

(d)   If the surety has good cause for surrendering the defendant and has complied with the provisions of this section in surrendering the defendant, there shall be no requirement that the surety return part or all of the premium paid for the bail bond.

History: Acts 1989, No. 417, § 5; 1995, No. 593, § 1; 1999, No. 1445, § 1; 2001, No. 1387, § 2.

§ 16-84-115. Deposit of money in lieu of bail[2]

Notwithstanding any rule of criminal procedure to the contrary:

(1)(A) Whenever the defendant is admitted to bail in a specified sum, he or she may deposit the sum with the proper city or county official in the city or county in which the trial is directed to be had and take from the official a receipt of the deposit, upon delivering which to the officer in whose custody he or she is, he or she shall be discharged.

(B)   After bail has been taken, a deposit may in like manner be made of the sum mentioned in the bail bond, which shall exonerate the surety.

---

[2] Statutes on procedure are subordinate to court rules.

(2)   Where money is deposited, the proper city or county official shall hold and pay the money according to the orders of the court having jurisdiction to try the offense, and he or she and his or her sureties shall be liable for the money on their official bond.

(3)   Upon judgment being rendered against a defendant for fine and costs, the court rendering judgment may order any money deposited agreeably to this section to be applied to the payment thereof. This subdivision (a)(3) shall not apply to a bail bond of a bail bondsman.

(4)   The mayor shall designate the city official or officials who may accept a deposit of money in lieu of bail, and the county judge shall designate the county official or officials authorized to accept a deposit of money in lieu of bail.

History: Acts 1989, No. 417, § 5; 1991, No. 720, § 1.

§ 16-84-116.   Recommitment after bail or deposit of money

(a)   The court in which a prosecution for a public offense is pending may, by an order, direct the defendant to be arrested and committed to jail until legally discharged, after he or she has given bail, or deposited money in lieu thereof, in the following cases:

(1)   When by having failed to appear, a forfeiture of bail or of the money deposited has been incurred;
(2)   When the court is satisfied that his or her surety, or either of them, is dead, or insufficient, or has moved from the state;
(3)   Upon an indictment's being found for an offense not bailable.

(b)   Upon the order being made, the clerk shall issue process for the arrest and recommitment of the defendant. If the order is made on account of either of the cases mentioned in subdivision (a)(1) or (a)(2) of this section, the defendant shall be admitted to bail as upon his or her first commitment, in a sum to be fixed by the court and named in the process for his or her arrest.

History: Acts 1989, No. 417, § 5.

16-84-201. Action on bond in district courts

(a)(1)(A) If the defendant fails to appear for trial or judgment, or at any other time when his or her presence in district court may be lawfully required, or to surrender himself or herself in execution of the judgment, the district court may direct the fact to be entered on the minutes and shall promptly issue an order requiring the surety to appear, on a date set by the district court not more than one hundred twenty (120) days from the date notice is sent by certified mail to the surety company at the address shown on the bond, whether or not it is received by the surety, to show cause why the sum specified in the bail bond or the money deposited in lieu of bail should not be forfeited.

(B) The one hundred twenty-day period in which the defendant must be surrendered or apprehended under subdivision (c)(2) of this section begins to run from the date notice is sent by certified mail to the surety company at the address shown on the bond, whether or not it is received by the surety.

(2) The order shall also require the officer who was responsible for taking of bail to appear unless:

(A) The surety is a bail bondsman; or

(B) The officer accepted cash in the amount of bail.

(b) The appropriate law enforcement agencies shall make every reasonable effort to apprehend the defendant.

(c)(1) If the defendant is surrendered or arrested, or good cause is shown for his or her failure to appear before judgment is entered against the surety, the district court shall exonerate a reasonable amount of the surety's liability under the bail bond.

(2) However, if the surety causes the apprehension of the defendant or the defendant is apprehended within one hundred twenty (120) days from the date notice is sent by certified mail to the surety company at the address shown on the bond, whether or not it is received by the surety, a judgment or forfeiture of bond may not be entered against the surety, except as provided in subsection (e) of this section.

(d) If after one hundred twenty (120) days from the date notice is sent by certified mail to the surety company at the address shown on the bond, whether or not it is received by the suety, the defendant has not surrendered or been arrested, the bail bond or money deposited in lieu of bail may be forfeited without further notice or hearing.

(e) If the defendant is located in another state and the location is known within one hundred twenty (120) days from the date notice is sent by, certified mail to the surety at the address shown on the bond, whether or not it is received by the surety, the appropriate law enforcement officers shall cause the arrest of the defendant and the surety shall be liable for the cost of returning the defendant to the district court in an amount not to exceed the face value of the bail bond.

(f)(1) In determining the extent of liability of the surety on a bond forfeiture, the court, without further notice or hearing, may take into consideration the expenses incurred by the surety in attempting to locate the defendant and may allow the surety credit for the expenses incurred.

(2) To be considered by the court, information concerning expenses incurred in attempting to locate the defendant should be submitted to the court by the surety no later than the one-hundred-twentieth day from the date notice is sent by certified mail to the surety company at the address shown on the bond, whether or not it is received by the surety.

(g) Notwithstanding any law to the contrary, a district court may suspend a bail bond company's or agent's ability to issue bail bonds in its court if the bail bond company or agent fails to comply with an order of the district court or fails to pay forfeited bonds in accordance with a district court's order.

History: Acts 1989, No. 417, § 5; 1991, No. 991, § 1; 1993, No. 841, § 1; 1995, No. 1106, § 1; 1999, No. 567, § 5; 2003, No. 752, § 2; 2003, No. 1572, § 1.

§ 16-84-202. Disposition of deposit

(a) Where money is deposited in lieu of bail with a city official, after the forfeiture and final judgment of the court, the city official shall make settlement with the city treasurer who shall deposit the funds to the credit of the city general fund.

(b) Where money is deposited in lieu of bail with a county official, after the forfeiture and final adjournment of the court, the county official shall make settlement with the county treasurer who shall deposit the funds to the credit of the county general fund.

History: Acts 1989, No. 417, § 5; 1991, No. 720, § 2.

§ 16-84-203. Certain absences excused

(a) No forfeiture of any appearance or bail bond shall be rendered in any case where a sworn statement of a licensed court-appointed physician is furnished the court showing that the principal in the bond is prevented from attending by some physical or mental disability or where a sworn affidavit of the jailer, warden, or other responsible officer of a jail or correctional facility in which the principal is being detained shall be furnished to the court, or a sworn affidavit of any officer in charge is furnished to the court showing that the principal in the bond is prevented from attending due to the fact that he or she is being detained by a force claiming to act under the authority of the federal government that neither the state nor the surety could control.

(b)   The appearance or bail bond shall remain in full force and effect until the principal is physically or mentally able to appear or until a detainer against the principal is filed with the detaining authority.

History: Acts 1989, No. 417, § 5; 2005, No. 1994, § 283.

§ 16-84-207. Action on bail bond in circuit courts

(a)   If a bail bond is granted by a judicial officer, it shall be conditioned on the defendant's appearing for trial, surrendering in execution of the judgment, or appearing at any other time when his or her presence in circuit court may be lawfully required under Rule 9.5 or Rule 9.6 of the Arkansas Rules of Criminal Procedure, or any other rule.

(b)(1) If the defendant fails to appear at any time when the defendant's presence is required under subsection (a) of this section, the circuit court shall enter this fact by written order or docket entry, adjudge the bail bond of the defendant or the money deposited in lieu thereof to be forfeited, and issue a warrant for the arrest of the defendant.

(2)   The circuit clerk shall:
(A)   Notify the sheriff and each surety on the bail bond that the defendant should be surrendered to the sheriff as required by the terms of the bail bond; and
(B)   Immediately issue a summons on each surety on the bail bond requiring the surety to personally appear on the date and time stated in the summons to show cause why judgment should not be rendered for the sum specified in the bail bond on account of the forfeiture.

(c)(1)(A) If the defendant is apprehended and brought before the circuit court within seventy-five (75) days of the date notification is sent under subdivision (b)(2)(A) of this section, then no judgment of forfeiture may be entered against the surety.
(B)   The surety shall be liable for the cost of returning the defendant to the circuit court in an amount not to exceed the face amount of the bond.

(2)(A) If the defendant is apprehended and brought before the circuit court after the seventy-five-day period under subdivision (c)(1) of this section, the circuit court may exonerate the amount of the surety's liability under the bail bond as the circuit court determines in its discretion and, if the surety does not object, enter judgment accordingly against the surety.[3]

(B) In determining the extent of liability of the surety on the bond, the circuit court may take into consideration the actions taken and the expenses incurred by the surety to locate the defendant, the expenses incurred by law enforcement officers to locate and return the defendant, and any other factors the circuit court finds relevant.

(3) The appropriate law enforcement agencies shall make every reasonable effort to apprehend the defendant.

(d)(1) If the surety does not consent to the entry of judgment in the amount determined under subsection (c) of this section, or if the defendant has not surrendered or been brought into custody, then at the time of the show cause hearing unless continued to a subsequent time, the circuit court shall determine the surety's liability and enter judgment on the forfeited bond.

(2) The circuit court may exercise its discretion in determining the amount of the judgment and may consider the factors listed in subsection (c) of this section.

(e)(1) No pleading on the part of the state shall be required in order to enforce a bond under this section.

(2) The summons required under subsection (b) of this section shall be made returnable and shall be executed as in civil actions, and the action shall be docketed and shall proceed as an ordinary civil action.

(3) The summons shall be directed to and served on the surety in the manner provided in Rule 4 of the Arkansas Rules of Civil Procedure, and the surety's appearance pursuant to the summons shall be in person and not by filing an answer or other pleading.

(f) Notwithstanding any law to the contrary, a circuit court may suspend a bail bond company's or agent's ability to issue bail bonds in its court if the bail bond company or agent fails to comply with an order of the circuit court or fails to pay forfeited bonds in accordance with a circuit court's order.

---

[3] Note: Under A.R.C.P. 60(a), Relief from judgment, decree or order, many courts will permit modification or vacating the judgment with 90 days: "To correct errors or mistakes or to prevent the miscarriage of justice, the court may modify or vacate a judgment, order or decree on motion of the court or any party, with prior notice to all parties, within ninety days of its having been filed with the clerk."

History: Acts 2003, No. 752, § 1; 2003, No. 1472, § 1.

§ 16-85-101. Right to attorney, physician, and phone calls

(a)   While confined and awaiting trial in any prison or jail in this state, no prisoner shall be denied the right to:
    (1)   Consult an attorney of the prisoner's own choosing;
    (2)   Call a physician of the prisoner's own choosing if in need of one; or
    (3)   Place free telephone calls to a bondsperson if the calls are local calls.

(b)   Any officer or other person having charge or supervision of any prisoner in the state who refuses to permit the prisoner to consult an attorney of the prisoner's own choosing, call a physician of the prisoner's own choosing, or place free telephone calls to a bondsperson if the calls are local shall be guilty of a Class B misdemeanor.

History: Acts 1937, No. 306, §§ 2, 3; Pope's Dig., §§ 3043, 3044; A.S.A. 1947, §§ 43-417.1, 43-417.2; Acts 2001, No. 1682, § 1; 2003, No. 1648, § 2; 2005, No. 1994, § 236.

§ 16-90-105. Verdict of guilty

(a)   Upon the return of a verdict of guilty, if tried by a jury, or the finding of guilt if tried by the circuit court without a jury, sentence may be announced.

(b)   The judgment of the court may be then and there entered for sentencing and the entry of the judgment may be postponed to a date certain then fixed by the court not more than thirty (30) days thereafter, at which time probation reports may be submitted, matters of mitigation presented, or any other matter heard that the court or the defendant might deem appropriate to consider before the pronouncement of sentence and entry of the formal judgment.

(c)   If the defendant is ordered to be held without bond or for any reason whatever, the defendant may file a written demand for immediate sentencing, whereupon the trial judge shall cause formal sentence and judgment to be made of record.

(d)   At the time sentence is announced and judgment entered, the trial judge must advise the defendant of his or her right to appeal and either fix or deny bond.

(e)   In its discretion, the trial judge may order:

(1)   The defendant released from custody on his or her own recognizance;

(2)   Another bond fixed;

(3)   The defendant to remain subject to the provisions of his or her bond if the defendant appeared at trial on bail bond; or

(4)   The defendant to the custody of the sheriff to be held without bond.

History: Acts 1971, No. 333, § 2; A.S.A. 1947, § 43-2301.

Chapter 94. Extradition

§ 16-94-216. Bail

Unless the offense with which the prisoner is charged is shown to be an offense punishable by death or life imprisonment under the laws of the state in which it was committed, the judge or magistrate must admit the person arrested to bail by bond or undertaking, with sufficient sureties, and in such sum as the judge or magistrate deems proper, for the prisoner's appearance before the judge or magistrate at a time specified in such bond or undertaking, and for the prisoner's surrender, to be arrested upon the warrant of the Governor of this state.

History: Acts 1935, No. 126, § 16; Pope's Dig., § 6096; A.S.A. 1947, § 43-3016.

§ 16-94-217. Discharge of warrant

If the accused is not arrested under warrant of the Governor by the expiration of the time specified in the warrant, bond, or undertaking, the judge or magistrate may discharge the accused or may recommit the accused to a further day, or may again take bail for his or her appearance and surrender, as provided in § 16-94-216; and at the expiration of the second period of commitment, or if the accused has been bailed and appeared according to the terms of his or her bond or undertaking, the judge or magistrate may either discharge the prisoner, or may require the prisoner to enter into a new bond or undertaking, to appear and surrender himself or herself at another day.

History: Acts 1935, No. 126, § 17; Pope's Dig., § 6097; A.S.A. 1947, § 43-3017.

Chapter 19. Bail Bondsmen

§ 17-19-101. Definitions

As used in this chapter, unless the context otherwise requires:

(1)   "Bail bond or appearance bond" means a bond for a specified monetary amount which is executed by the defendant and a qualified licensee under this chapter and which is issued to a court, magistrate, or authorized officer as security for the subsequent court appearance of the defendant upon his or her release from actual custody pending the appearance;

(2)   "Board" means the Professional Bail Bond Company and Professional Bail Bondsman Licensing Board;

(3)   "Insurer" means any surety company which has qualified to transact surety business in this state;

(4)   "Licensee" means a professional bail bond company or a professional bail bondsman;

(5)   "Professional bail bond company" means an individual who is a resident of this state, an Arkansas firm, partnership, or corporation, or a foreign corporation registered and authorized to conduct business in the State of Arkansas that pledges a bail bond in connection with a judicial proceeding and receives or is promised therefor money or other things of value; and

(6)   "Professional bail bondsman" means an individual who is a resident of this state and who acts through authority of a professional bail bond company in pledging a bail bond as security in a judicial proceeding.

History: Acts 1989, No. 417, § 1; 1995, No. 827, §§ 1, 3.

§ 17-19-102. Penalties

(a)   Any person who is found guilty of violating any of the provisions of this chapter shall upon conviction be guilty of a Class A misdemeanor.

(b)   Any person who falsely represents to the Professional Bail Bond Company and Professional Bail Bondsman Licensing Board that any person has met the education or continuing education requirements of §§ 17-19-107, 17-19-212, and 17-19-401 et seq., shall be guilty of a Class B misdemeanor and upon conviction shall be punished accordingly.

History: Acts 1989, No. 417, § 1; 1993, No. 499, § 6; 2005, No. 1994, § 226.

§ 17-19-103. Civil and criminal proceedings

The venue for any criminal or civil proceeding filed for any violation of this chapter shall be in the county wherein the violation occurred.

History: Acts 1989, No. 417, § 1.

§ 17-19-104. Exemption

This chapter shall not affect the negotiation through a licensed broker or agent for, nor the execution or delivery of, an undertaking of bail executed by an insurer for its insured under a policy of automobile insurance or of liability insurance upon the automobile of the insured.

History: Acts 1989, No. 417, § 1.

§ 17-19-105. Prohibitions

No professional bail bondsman or professional bail bond company, nor court, nor law enforcement officer, nor any individual working on behalf of a professional bail bondsman or professional bail bond company, shall:
(1)   Require as a condition of his or her executing a bail bond that the principal agree to engage the services of a specified attorney;
(2)   Solicit business or advertise for business in or about any place where prisoners are confined or in or about any court;
(3)   Suggest or advise the engagement of any bail bond company or professional bail bondsman to underwrite a bail bond;
(4)   Enter a police station, jail, sheriff's office, or other place where persons in custody of the law are detained for the purpose of obtaining employment as a professional bail bondsman or professional bail bond company, without having been previously called by a person so detained or by some relative or other authorized person acting for or in behalf of the person so detained. Whenever such an entry occurs, the person in charge of the facility shall be given, and promptly record, the mission of the licensee and the name of the person calling the licensee and requesting him or her to

come;

(5)   Pay a fee or rebate or give or promise anything of value to:

(A)   A jailer, policeman, peace officer, committing magistrate, or any other person who has power to arrest or to hold in custody; or

(B)   Any public official or public employee in order to secure a settlement, compromise, remission, or reduction of the amount of any bail bond or estreatment thereof;

(6)   Pay a fee or rebate or give anything of value to an attorney in bail bond matters, except in defense of any action on a bond;

(7)   Pay a fee or rebate or give or promise anything of value to the principal or anyone in his or her behalf;

(8)(A) Participate in the capacity of an attorney at a trial or hearing of one on whose bond he or she is surety;

(B)   Attempt to obtain settlement or dismissal of a case;

(C)   Give or attempt to give any legal advice to one on whose bond he or she is surety; or

(9)   Accept anything of value from a principal except the premium, provided that the licensee shall be permitted to accept collateral security or other indemnity from the principal which shall be returned upon final termination of liability on the bond. The collateral security or other indemnity required by the licensee must be reasonable in relation to the amount of the bond.

History: Acts 1989, No. 417, § 1; 1997, No. 973, § 5.

§ 17-19-106.   Professional Bail Bond Company and Professional Bail Bondsman Licensing Board

(a)   This section may be cited as the "Arkansas Professional Bail Bond Company and Professional Bail Bondsman Licensing Act".

(b)(1) There is hereby created the Professional Bail Bond Company and Professional Bail Bondsman Licensing Board.

(2)(A) The board shall be composed of eight (8) members to be appointed by the Governor for terms of seven (7) years,

(B)   Vacancies shall be filled by appointment of the Governor for the unexpired portion of the term.

(3)(A) Three (3) members of the board shall be licensed bail bond company owners, one (1) a municipal chief of police, one (1) a county sheriff, one (1) a municipal or circuit judge, and two (2) shall be a residents of the state who are not a bail bond company owner, elected judge, sheriff, or chief of police.

(B)(i) No two (2) of the three (3) bail bondsman members shall reside in the same congressional district.

(ii)   At least one (1) board member shall be an African-American.

(iii)   At least one (1) board member shall be a female.

(4)   The board shall have the authority and responsibility to administer and enforce the provisions of this chapter relating to licensing and regulation of professional bail bond companies and professional bail bondsmen.

(5)   The board shall have the authority to adopt and enforce such reasonable rules and regulations as it shall determine to be necessary to enable it to effectively and efficiently carry out its official duty of licensing and regulating professional bail bond companies and professional bail bondsmen.

(c)   The members of the board shall receive expense reimbursement in accordance with § 25-16-901 et seq., and a stipend pursuant to § 25-16-904.(d)The provisions of this section shall not be construed to repeal any laws in effect on August 13, 1993, relating to the licensing and regulation of professional bail bond companies and professional bail bondsmen but such laws shall remain in full force and effect and shall be administered by the board created herein.

History: Acts 1993, No. 500, §§ 1-5; 1995, No. 827, § 2; 1997, No. 250, § 126; 1999, No. 1286, § 2; 2001, No. 1817, § 1.

§ 17-19-107. exception to education requirements

Any licensed professional bail bondsman who is sixty-five (65) years of age or older and who has been licensed as a bail bondsman for fifteen (15) years or more shall be exempt from both the education and continuing education requirements of § 17-19-212 and § 17-19-401 et seq.

History: Acts 1993, No. 499, § 3.

§ 17-19-108. Rules and regulations

The Professional Bail Bond Company and Professional Bail Bondsman Licensing Board shall adopt such reasonable rules and regulations as it shall deem necessary to assure the effective and efficient administration of §§ 17-19-107, 17-19-212, and 17-19-401 et seq.

History: Acts 1993, No. 499, § 7.

§ 17-19-109. Advertising by professional bail bond companies

(a)   All business cards, signs, telephone ads, newspaper ads, or any other type f advertising by professional bail bond companies shall display the company name prominently to assure that the identity of the company doing the advertising is readily apparent.

(b)   Any such advertising by or on behalf of individual professional bail bondsmen shall prominently display the name of the bail bond company and shall contain no information or other indication that the bail bondsman is independent of the company.

History: Acts 1993, No. 400, § 1.

§ 17-19-110. Licensed bail bond agent

(a)   A licensed bail bond agent shall be permitted to write a bail bond in any county with a current copy of his or her license if:
(1)   The agent has a current license with a current licensed professional bail bond company; and
(2)   The agent and the agent's company are in good standing with the courts in the jurisdiction where the bond is to be posted.

(b)   A licensed bail bond agent shall carry a current copy of his or her company's license, his or her bail bond agent license, and a current copy of his or her qualifying power of attorney that is on file with the Professional Bail Bond Company and Professional Bail Bondsman Licensing Board.

(c)(1) Only one (1) power of attorney per bond not exceeding the agent's qualifying power of attorney shall be permitted unless a court has separated the charges and amounts of bonds.
(2)   Powers of attorney shall not be stacked.

History: Acts 1993, No. 402, § 1; 1999, No. 567, § 2; 2003, No. 1648, § 3.

§ 17-19-111. Fees

(a)   Notwithstanding any other provisions of this chapter to the contrary, and notwithstanding any other provisions of Arkansas law to the contrary, professional bail bond companies are hereby required to charge, collect, and remit the following fees for direct deposit as special revenues into the State Insurance Department Trust Fund for the support, personnel, maintenance, and operations of the State Insurance Department and for the Domestic Peace Fund administered by the Arkansas Child Abuse/Rape/ Domestic Violence Commission, in addition to any other fees, taxes, premium taxes, levies, or other assessments imposed in connection with the issuance of bail bonds by professional bail bond companies under Arkansas law.

(b)(1) In addition to the bail or appearance bond premium or compensation allowed under § 17-19-301, each licensed professional bail bond company shall charge and collect as a nonrefundable fee for the fund an additional ten-dollar fee per bail bond for giving bond for each and every bail and appearance bond issued by the licensed professional bail bond company by or through its individual licensees.

(2)   The fees shall be collected quarterly and then reported and filed with the Insurance Commissioner no later than fifteen (15) calendar days after the end of each quarter.

(3)   The notarized quarterly reporting form and a notarized annual reconciliation form as to all fees collected for the fund shall be filed by each professional bail bond company on forms prescribed by the commissioner and at the times and in the manner as the commissioner shall prescribe in conformity with this section.

(4)   A paper-processing charge of fifteen dollars ($15.00) shall be collected on each bail bond in order to defray the surety's costs incurred by the quarterly and annual reporting requirements contained herein and to further defray the surety's costs incurred in the collection of all fees due, owing, and collected on behalf of the fund and the surety's costs incurred in the preparation of all required reports submitted in conformance with the standards established by the American Institute of Certified Public Accountants.

(c)(1) The commissioner may, in his or her discretion, grant an extension for the filing of the report and fees for good cause shown upon timely written request.

(2)   Absent an extension for good cause shown, each licensed professional bail bond company failing to report or pay these fees shall be liable to the fund for a monetary penalty of one hundred dollars ($100) per day for each day of delinquency.

(3)   The commissioner may pursue any appropriate legal remedies on behalf of the fund to collect any delinquent fees and penalties owed as special revenues.

(d)(1) Upon collection of the fees and any monetary penalties, the commissioner shall deposit as special revenues:

(A)   Sufficient fees and penalties directly into the State Insurance Department Trust Fund to provide for the personal services and operating expenses of the Professional Bail Bond Company and Professional Bail Bondsman Licensing Board under subsection (g) of this section; and

(B)   The remainder of all fees and penalties directly into the Domestic Peace Fund administered by the Arkansas Child Abuse/Rape/Domestic Violence Commission.

(2)   The fees and penalties shall be in addition to all other fees, licensure or registration fees, taxes, assessments, levies, or penalties payable to any federal or state office, court, agency, board, or commission or other public official or officer of the state, or its political subdivisions, including counties, cities, or municipalities, by professional bail bond companies.

(3)(A)   Each individual bail bondsman is required to assist in collection of the fees but is exempt from the duty and responsibility of payment of the fees to the fund unless he or she misappropriates or converts such moneys to his or her own use or to the use of others not entitled to the fees.

(B)   In that case, the commissioner shall proceed on behalf of the fund with any civil or criminal remedies at his or her disposal against the individual responsible.

(C)   Upon criminal conviction of the individual responsible for fraudulent conversion of the moneys due the fund, the individual responsible shall pay restitution to the trust fund, and the court shall incorporate a finding to that effect in its order.

(D)   Absent substantial evidence to the contrary, the violations of the individual may be attributed to the employing bail bond company, and any criminal or civil court may, in its discretion and upon substantial evidence, order the employing bail bond company to pay restitution to the fund on behalf of the responsible individual and shall incorporate that finding into its order.

(e)   For purposes of any statutory security deposit Arkansas law requires of professional bail bond companies, including, but not limited to, the deposit under § 17-19-205, the payment of the fees required by this section is considered to be a duty of the licensee, so as to allow the commissioner on behalf of the fund to make a claim against any such deposit for the fees required by this section and any penalties owed thereon, up to the limit of any security deposit.

(f)   Under no circumstances shall the fees or penalties thereon held in or for deposit into the fund as special revenues be subject to any tax, levy, or assessment of any kind, including, but not limited to, any bond forfeiture claims, any garnishment or general creditors' claims, any remedies under Title 16 of this Code, or other provisions of Arkansas law.

(g)(1) At the beginning of each fiscal year, the department shall certify to the Chief Fiscal Officer of the State an amount sufficient to provide for personal services and operating expenses of the Professional Bail Bond Company and Professional Bail

Bondsman Licensing Board.

(2)   The Chief Fiscal Officer of the State shall then transfer the certified amount from the State Insurance Department Trust Fund to the Bail Bondsman Board Fund.

History: Acts 1993, No. 901, § 31; 1997, No. 1096, § 1; 1997, No. 1248, § 39; 2007, No. 730, § 1.

§ 17-19-201. Licenses required

(a)   No person shall engage in bail bond business without first having been licensed as provided in this chapter.

(b)   A professional bail bondsman shall not execute or issue an appearance bond in this state without holding a valid appointment from a professional bail bond company and without attaching to the appearance bond an executed and numbered power of attorney referencing the professional bail bond company.

(c)   An insurer shall not execute an undertaking of bail without being licensed as a professional bail bond company.

(d)   A professional bail bond company shall not engage in the bail bond business:
(1)   Without having been licensed as a professional bail bond company under this chapter; and
(2)   Except through an agent licensed as a professional bail bondsman under this chapter.

(e)   A professional bail bond company shall not permit any unlicensed person to solicit or engage in the bail bond business in the company's behalf, except for individuals who are employed solely for the performance of clerical, stenographic, investigative, or other administrative duties which do not require a license under this chapter and whose compensation is not related to or contingent upon the number of bonds written.

History: Acts 1989, No. 417, § 1.

§ 17-19-202. Applications

(a) Every applicant for a professional bail bondsman license or a professional bail bond company license shall apply on forms furnished by the Professional Bail Bond Company and Professional Bail Bondsman Licensing Board.

(b) The application of a professional bail bondsman shall be accompanied by a duly executed power of attorney issued by the professional bail bond company for whom the professional bail bondsman will be acting.

(c)(1) An application for a professional bail bond company license shall be accompanied by proof that the applicant:

(A) Is an Arkansas partnership, firm, or corporation, a foreign corporation registered and authorized to conduct business in the State of Arkansas, or an individual who is a resident of the state; and

(B) Has at least one (1) owner or partner that has been licensed for at least two (2) years during the last three (3) years by the State of Arkansas as a professional bail bondsman.

(2) A corporation shall file proof that its most recent annual franchise tax has been paid to the Secretary of State.

(D)(1)(A) At the time of application for every professional bail bond company license, there shall be paid to the board:

(i) For a new company license, a fee of two thousand five hundred dollars ($2,500); or

(ii) For a renewal of a company license, a fee of one thousand dollars ($1,000).

(B) Each professional bail bond company license or renewal for a sole proprietor, partnership, or corporation shall include one (1) license for one (1) agent per company per year.

(2) Each applicant for a professional bail bondsman license shall pay the board a license fee of one hundred dollars ($100) at the time of application, except that if the applicant is also an applicant as an individual for a professional bail bond company license, then the applicant shall not be required to pay a license fee for licensure as a professional bail bondsman but shall comply with all other requirements for licensure as a professional bail bondsman.

(3) License fees shall be payable in full on a yearly basis regardless of the date of issuance.

(4) Any agent who transfers his or her license from one professional bail bond company to another shall:

(A) Pay to the board a transfer fee of two hundred fifty dollars ($250); and

(B) File with the board:

(i)   A sworn affidavit stating that all premiums, fees, and powers of attorney owed to or issued by the professional bail bond company from which he or she is transferring his or her license have been delivered to the company;

(ii)   A letter of resignation addressed to the professional bail bond company from which he or she is transferring or a letter of termination addressed to him or her from the professional bail bond company terminating his or her appointment;

(iii)   A completed agent application on forms prescribed by the board;

(iv)   A completed company statement from the company to which he or she desires to transfer his or her license; and

(v)   An original qualifying power of attorney issued by the company to which he or she desires to transfer his or her license.

(5)(A) Upon receipt of a request for transfer of a bail bondsman license, the applicable transfer fee, and the documents specified in subdivision (d)(4) of this section, the board shall forward copies of the letter of resignation, if applicable, and the sworn affidavit of the agent to the professional bail bond company from which the agent desires to transfer his or her license.

(B)   Upon receipt of the letter of resignation, if applicable, and the sworn affidavit of the licensee, the professional bail bond company from which the agent is transferring shall have seven (7) business days to contest the agent's sworn statement.

(C)   A professional bail bond company contesting an agent's sworn statement shall file a written complaint on forms furnished by the board setting out in detail the property that the company denies the agent has returned as attested by the sworn affidavit.

(D)   Any documents supporting the complaint contesting the sworn affidavit and which shall be offered as evidence to prove the complaint shall be filed with the complaint.

(E)   Upon receipt of the complaint, the Executive Director of the Professional Bail Bond Company and Professional Bail Bondsman Licensing Board shall set the matter for informal hearing to be held within seven (7) days of receipt of the complaint and advise the professional bail bond company and the agent by certified mail, return receipt requested, of the date, time, and location of the informal hearing.

(F)   Either party may appeal the decision of the executive director to a formal hearing before the board by filing with the board a notice of appeal within seven (7) days of receipt of the decision by the executive director.

(G)(i) No transfer of an agent's license shall be effective prior to the expiration of the seven-day period for contesting the transfer request unless the professional bail bond company from which the agent is requesting a transfer shall notify the board that it has no objection to the transfer, in which case the transfer may be entered prior to expiration of the seven-day period.

(ii)   If no complaint contesting the agent's sworn affidavit is received during the seven-day contest period, the license shall be transferred as requested.

(iii)   A professional bail bond company that does not contest the sworn affidavit of a transferring agent is not precluded by the failure to contest the sworn affidavit from filing a complaint that alleges a violation of the applicable statutes, rules, or regulations by the transferring agent upon discovery of the alleged violation by the professional bail bond company.

(H)(i) If the allegations of a complaint contesting the transfer are found by the board to have been established, no transfer of the license shall be accomplished until the agent accounts for, returns, or pays to the professional bail bond company contesting the transfer the property or money issued to or held in a fiduciary capacity by the agent.

(ii) If a complaint is filed contesting the sworn affidavit of the transferring agent, a specific finding of fact shall be made by the board concerning whether the affidavit or complaint contesting the affidavit was filed in good faith by the respective parties.

(iii) In the case of a finding of a lack of good faith, the party to whom the finding applies shall be subject to sanctions or disciplinary action pursuant to the provisions of § 17-19-210 and as provided by applicable rules.

History: Acts 1989, No. 417, § 1; 1995, No. 827, § 4; 1999, No. 567, § 1; 2001, No. 1680, § 1; 2005, No. 858, § 1; 2005, No. 1960, § 1.

§ 17-19-203. Character references

Each applicant for a professional bail bondsman license shall:

(1) File with the Professional Bail Bond Company and Professional Bail Bondsman Licensing Board written statements from at least three (3) persons who know his or her character;

(2)(A) Be required to apply to the Identification Bureau of the Department of Arkansas State Police for a state and nationwide criminal records check to be conducted by the Federal Bureau of Investigation.

(B) The criminal records check shall conform to the applicable federal standards and shall include the taking of fingerprints.

(C) The applicant shall sign a release of information to the board and shall be responsible to the Department of Arkansas State Police for the payment of any fee associated with the criminal records check.

(D) Upon completion of the criminal records check, the Identification Bureau of the Department of Arkansas State Police shall forward all information obtained concerning the applicant to the board.

(E) At the conclusion of the criminal background check required by this subdivision (2), the Identification Bureau of the Department of Arkansas State Police shall promptly destroy the fingerprint card of the applicant; and

(3)   Such other proof as the board may require that he or she is competent, trustworthy, financially responsible, and of good personal and business reputation and has not been convicted of a felony or any offense involving moral turpitude.

History: Acts 1989, No. 417, § 1; 1995, No. 827, § 4; 1999, No. 1346, § 1.

§ 17-19-204. Examination

(a)   In order to determine the competence of each applicant for a professional bail bondsman license, the Professional Bail Bond Company and Professional Bail Bondsman Licensing Board shall require every individual to submit to, and to pass to the satisfaction of the board, a written examination to be prepared by the board and appropriate to the transaction of bail bond business.

(b)   Such an examination shall be held in a location and at such times as the board shall determine.

(c)   Every individual applying to take a written examination shall, at the time of applying therefor, pay to the board a nonrefundable examination fee of twenty-five dollars ($25.00).

(d)   If the application is approved, and if the nonrefundable examination fee is paid, an examination permit will be issued to the applicant. The permit will be valid for a period of ninety (90) days from the date of issuance. If the applicant does not schedule and appear for examination within that ninety-day period, the permit shall expire and the applicant may be required to file a new application, and shall pay another nonrefundable examination fee of twenty-five dollars ($25.00) before issuance of another examination permit to the applicant.

(e)   If the applicant appears for examination but fails to pass the examination, the applicant may apply for reexamination. The reexamination fee shall be a nonrefundable fee of fifteen dollars ($15.00). The board may require a waiting period of eight (8) weeks before reexamination of an applicant who twice failed to pass previous similar examinations.

History: Acts 1989, No. 417, § 1; 1995, No. 827, § 4.

§ 17-19-205.   Letter of credit or certificate of deposit required

(a)(1) An applicant for a professional bail bond company license shall file with the Professional Bail Bond Company and Professional Bail Bondsman Licensing Board an irrevocable letter of credit from an Arkansas chartered bank or a federally chartered bank in Arkansas or a certificate of deposit.

(2)(A) The letter of credit or certificate of deposit shall be approved by the board as to form and sufficiency and shall be conditioned upon faithful performance of the duties of the licensee.

(B)   The minimum amount for a professional bail bond company initially licensed on or before July 1, 2009, shall be two hundred fifty thousand dollars ($250,000.00).

(C)   The minimum amount for any professional bail bond company initially licensed after July 1, 1989, shall be one hundred thousand dollars ($100,000).

(D)   Professional bail bond companies and professional bail bondsmen who were licensed under Act 400 of 1971 [repealed] prior to March 8, 1989, shall only be required to file or have on file with the board a letter of credit or certificate of deposit approved by the board as to form and sufficiency, in a minimum amount of five thousand dollars ($5,000), conditioned upon the faithful performance of the duties of the licensee, provided they do not exceed the maximum amount of unsecured bond commitments as provided in § 17-19-304.

(b)   No letter of credit or certificate of deposit shall be subject to termination or cancellation by either party in less than sixty (60) days after the giving of written notice thereof to the other parties and to the board.

(c)   No termination or cancellation shall affect the liability of the surety or sureties on a bond incurred prior to the effective date of termination or cancellation.

History: Acts 1989, No. 417, § 1; 1995, No. 827, § 4.

§ 17-19-206.   Duties of board and clerks

(a)   Before issuance of a license under the provisions of this chapter, every applicant for a license shall satisfy the Professional Bail Bond Company and Professional Bail Bondsman Licensing Board as to Arkansas residency, trustworthiness, and competence, as applicable, and shall otherwise comply with the conditions and qualifications set forth in this chapter.

(b)(1) The board may refuse to issue any license to an applicant who fails to comply with the provisions of this chapter or rule or regulation of the board.

(2)   The board may refuse to issue any such license to any applicant that has made a material misrepresentation in the application for such a license.

(c)   Upon the approval and issuance of any license provided for under this chapter, the board shall give written notice to the sheriff and circuit clerk of each county in the state.

(d)   Upon revocation or suspension of license, the board shall give written notice to that effect to the sheriff and circuit clerk in each county in the state.

(e)   The board shall maintain a complete record of registrations, revocations, and suspensions, and the record shall be available to the sheriff and county clerk of each county of the state.

(f)   Annually, the board shall furnish the sheriffs and circuit clerks with a list of renewal licenses.

History: Acts 1989, No. 417, § 1; 1995, No. 827, § 4; 2007, No. 674, § 1.

§ 17-19-207. Expiration and renewal

(a)   Every license issued pursuant to this chapter shall be for a term expiring on December 31 following the date of its issuance, and it may be renewed for the ensuing calendar year upon the filing of a renewal application.

(b)   The Professional Bail Bond Company and Professional Bail Bondsman Licensing Board may refuse to renew a license for any cause for which issuance of the original license could have been refused or for the licensee's violation of any of the provisions of this chapter or the rules and regulations of the board.

(c)   Every licensee shall be required to file a renewal application, the form and subject matter of which shall be prescribed by the board.

(d)(1) At the time of application for renewal of a professional bail bond company license, there shall be paid to the board for the company's renewal license a fee of one thousand dollars ($1,000).

(2)   Each professional bail bondsman shall pay a fee of one hundred dollars ($100) for renewal of the license, except that if the applicant for renewal also holds a professional bail bond company license, then the applicant shall not be required to pay a

renewal fee for a professional bail bondsman license.

History: Acts 1989, No. 417, § 1; 1995, No. 827, § 4.

§ 17-19-208. Civil action — Administrative action

(a)(1) If during the term of the letter of credit or certificate of deposit any licensee shall be guilty of misconduct or malfeasance in his or her dealings with any court or magistrate or officer or with any person or company in connection with any deposit or bail bond, the Professional Bail Bond Company and Professional Bail Bondsman Licensing Board may maintain a civil action on the letter of credit or certificate of deposit, or may maintain an administrative action on any certificate of deposit. The board may recover for the use and benefit of the person or persons aggrieved a maximum amount of ten thousand dollars ($10,000). The provisions of this subdivision (a)(1) shall be in addition to all other remedies available to the aggrieved person and nothing in this subdivision (a)(1) shall be construed as limiting the liability of a professional bail bond company or a professional bail bondsman.

(2) The board may suspend the license of such a licensee until such time as the board recovers the full amount allowable or recovers for the benefit of the persons aggrieved the amount of loss or injury sustained pursuant to subdivision (a)(1) of this section, and until such time as the licensee has filed with the board an additional letter of credit or certificate of deposit in the required amount. The board shall promptly notify the licensee as provided in subdivision (b)(2) of this section.

(b)(1) When a final civil judgment for court-ordered bond forfeitures is entered as to a bail bond issued by the licensee by a court of competent jurisdiction in this state and the judgment is not paid within ninety (90) days thereafter, the court may send a copy of the judgment, duly certified by the clerk of the court, and proof of service of the judgement on the licensee in accordance with Rule 5 of the Arkansas Rules of Civil Procedure to the board, then the board may promptly make a claim on the surety for payment of the allowable amount of the licensee's letters of credit on behalf of the court or shall withdraw the allowable amount of the licensee's certificates of deposit and shall transmit to the clerk of the court so much of the securities as are allowable. The board shall honor the judgments from the respective courts up to the limits set out in subdivision (a)(1) of this section.

(2) Upon receipt of the judgment and proof of notice of service on the licensee, the board may suspend the license of the licensee until such time as the judgment is paid or otherwise satisfied and until such time as the licensee has filed with the board another letter of credit or certificate of deposit in the required amount. The board shall promptly notify the licensee in writing by certified mail of the claims upon the

licensee's letter of credit or certificates of deposit and shall also include a copy of the board's order of suspension.

(3)　If the allowable amount of the letter of credit or certificate of deposit filed with the board is not sufficient to pay or otherwise satisfy the judgments as to bail bonds issued by the professional bail bond company in § 17-19-205(a), the board may promptly make a claim against the professional bail bond company on behalf of the court.

(c)　In the event a professional bail bond company fails to file with the board the additional letter of credit or certificate of deposit to maintain the license within ninety (90) days from the effective date of the board's order of suspension as provided in subdivisions (a)(2), (b)(2), or (b)(3) of this section, the board shall cancel the license of the licensee and shall promptly notify the licensee as provided in subdivision (b)(2) of this section.

(d)　Upon the nonrenewal, cancellation, or revocation of any license hereunder, the board will release to the licensee the qualifying bonds or certificates of deposit filed with the board only upon receipt of written documentation from all the courts in all the counties in which the licensee engaged in business that all bonds issued by the licensee have been exonerated, and that no unpaid bond forfeitures remain outstanding, and that all civil judgments as to forfeitures on bonds issued by the licensee have been paid in full.

(e)　If a company license has been revoked because of unpaid judgments, during the appeals process the company shall file a supersedeas bond in the amount of the unpaid judgments with the court in which the appeal is taken.

History: Acts 1989, No. 417, § 1; 1995, No. 827, § 4; 2001, No. 1679, § 1.

§ 17-19-209. Violations — Hearings

(a)　The Professional Bail Bond Company and Professional Bail Bondsman Licensing Board shall investigate any alleged violation of this chapter.

(b)　Any person may file a complaint stating facts constituting an alleged violation of this chapter. The complaint shall be signed under penalty of perjury.

(c)　All hearings held under this chapter shall be conducted in the same manner as hearings held by the board under the Arkansas Administrative Procedure Act, § 25-15-201 et seq., unless otherwise stated in this chapter.

(d)(1) With respect to the subject of any examination, investigation, or hearing being conducted by the board, the board may subpoena witnesses and administer oaths and affirmations, and examine any individual under oath, and may require and compel the production of records, books, papers, contracts, and other documents.

(2) Subpoenas of witnesses shall be served in the same manner as if issued by a circuit court and may be served by certified mail.

(3) If any individual fails to obey a subpoena issued and served pursuant to this section with respect to any matter concerning which he or she may be lawfully interrogated, upon application of the board, the Pulaski County Circuit Court may issue an order requiring the individual to comply with the subpoena and to testify.

(4) Any failure to obey the order of the court may be punished by the court as a contempt thereof.

(5) Any person willfully testifying falsely under oath to any matter material to any examination, investigation, or hearing shall upon conviction be guilty of perjury and punished accordingly.

(e) Not less than ten (10) days in advance, the board shall give notice of the time and place of the hearing, stating the matters to be considered at the hearing.

(f) The board shall allow any party to the hearing to appear in person and by counsel, to be present during the giving of all evidence, to have a reasonable opportunity to inspect all documentary evidence and to examine witnesses, to present evidence in support of his or her interest, and to have subpoenas issued by the board to compel attendance of witnesses and production of evidence in his or her behalf.

(g)(1) A party may appeal from any order of the board as a matter of right and shall be taken to the Pulaski County Circuit Court by filing written notice of appeal to the court and by filing a copy of the notice with the board.

(2) Within thirty (30) days after filing the copy of a notice of appeal with the board, the board shall make, certify, and deposit in the office of the clerk of the court in which the appeal is pending a full and complete transcript of all proceedings had before the board and all evidence before the board in the matter, including all of the board's files therein.

History: Acts 1989, No. 417, § 1; 1995, No. 827, § 4; 1997, No. 973, § 6; 1999, No. 1477, § 1; 2003, No. 1174, § 1.

§ 17-19-210. Suspension — Review

(a) The Professional Bail Bond Company and Professional Bail Bondsman Licensing Board may suspend for up to twelve (12) months or revoke or refuse to continue any license issued pursuant to the provisions of this chapter if, after notice and hearing, the board determines that the licensee or any member of a company which is so licensed has:

(1) Violated any provision of, or any obligation imposed by, this chapter or any lawful rule, regulation, or order of the board or has been convicted of a felony or any offense involving moral turpitude;

(2) Made a material misstatement in the application for license, in the application for renewal license, or in the financial statement which accompanies the application or renewal application for license as a professional bail bond company;

(3) Committed any fraudulent or dishonest acts or practices or demonstrated his or her incompetency or untrustworthiness to act as such a licensee;

(4) Charged or received, as premium or compensation for the making of any deposit or bail bond, any sum in excess of that permitted by law;

(5) Required as a condition of his or her executing a bail bond that the principal agree to engage the services of a specified attorney;

(6) Signed, executed, or issued bonds with endorsements in blank, or prepared or issued fraudulent or forged bonds or power of attorney;

(7) Failed in the applicable regular course of business to account for and to pay premiums held by the licensee in a fiduciary capacity to the professional bail bond company or other person entitled thereto; or

(8) Failed to comply with the provisions of the laws of this state, or rule, regulation, or order of the board for which issuance of the license could have been refused had it then existed and been known to the board.

(b) The acts or conduct of any professional bail bondsman who acts within the scope of the authority delegated to him or her shall also be deemed the act or conduct of the professional bail bond company for which the professional bail bondsman is acting as agent.

(c) If the board finds that one (1) or more grounds exist for the suspension or revocation of any license, the board may in its discretion request that formal charges be filed against the violator and that penalties set out in § 17-19-102 be imposed.

(d) If the board finds that one (1) or more grounds exist for the suspension or revocation of a license and that the license has been suspended within the previous twenty-four (24) months, then the board shall revoke the license.

(e) The board may not again issue a license under this chapter to any person or entity whose license has been revoked.

(f)   If the board determines that the public health, safety, or welfare impera-
tively requires emergency action, and incorporates a finding to that effect in its order, a
summary suspension of a license issued pursuant to this chapter may be ordered pending
an administrative hearing before the board, which shall be promptly instituted.

(g)   If a professional bail bond company license is so suspended or revoked, no
member of the company or officer or director of the corporation shall be licensed or be
designated in any license to exercise the powers thereof during the period of the suspension or revocation, unless the board determines upon substantial evidence that the member, officer, or director was not personally at fault and did not acquiesce in the matter on
account of which the license was suspended or revoked.

(h)   The action of the board in issuing or refusing to issue or in suspending or
revoking any license shall be subject to review by the Circuit Court of Pulaski County
upon filing of an action therefor within thirty (30) days after the issuance of written
notice by the board of the action taken.

History: Acts 1989, No. 417, § 1; 1995, No. 827, § 4.

§ 17-19-211. Administrative penalty

If the Professional Bail Bond Company and Professional Bail Bondsman Licensing Board finds that one (1) or more grounds exist for the suspension or revocation of
any license, the board in its discretion, and in lieu of suspension or revocation, may
impose upon the licensee an administrative penalty in an amount not to exceed five
thousand dollars ($5,000).

History: Acts 1989, No. 417, § 1; 1995, No. 827, § 5; 1997, No. 973, § 7.

§ 17-19-212. Licenses

Each applicant for an initial bail bondsman license who satisfactorily completes
the examination and meets the other qualifications and requirements prescribed by law,
including the completion of a minimum of eight (8) hours of education in subjects
pertaining to the authority and responsibilities of a bail bondsman and a review of the
laws and regulations relating thereto, shall be licensed by the Professional Bail Bond

Company and Professional Bail Bondsman Licensing Board.

History: Acts 1993, No. 499, § 1; 1997, No. 973, § 8; 1999, No. 567, § 3.

§ 17-19-301. Premiums

(a)   With the exception of other provisions of this section, the premium or compensation for giving bond or depositing money or property as bail on any bond shall be ten percent (10%), except that the amount may be rounded up to the nearest five-dollar amount.

(b)   The minimum compensation for giving bond or depositing money or property as bail on any bond shall be not less than fifty dollars ($50.00).

(c)   If a bail bond or appearance bond issued by a licensee under this chapter must be replaced with another bail bond or appearance bond because of the licensee's violation of any provision of the laws of this state or any rule, regulation, or order of the Professional Bail Bond Company and Professional Bail Bondsman Licensing Board, the licensee who violated the provision and who caused the replacement to be required shall pay all the premium amount for the replacement bond, in an amount not to exceed the amount of the original bond, without any contribution from the respective defendant or principal.

(d)(1)(A) In addition to the ten percent (10%) bail or appearance bond premium or compensation allowed in subsection (a) of this section, and commencing on April 1, 1993, each licensed professional bail bond company shall charge and collect as a nonrefundable administrative and regulatory fee for the State Insurance Department Trust Fund an additional ten dollars ($10.00) per bond fee for giving bond for every bail and appearance bond issued by the licensed professional bail bond company by or through its individual licensees.

(B)   The administrative and regulatory fees payable by these companies to the fund for the support and operation of the department, and collected by the bail bond companies as required by this section, shall be reported and filed with the Insurance Commissioner no later than fifteen (15) calendar days after the end of each calendar quarter, contemporaneous with the professional bail bond company's filing of its quarterly bail bond report with the department.

(C)   A notarized annual reconciliation of all such fees collected in the preceding calendar year for the fund shall be filed by each licensed professional bail bond company at a time and on forms prescribed by the commissioner.

(D)   The commissioner may in his or her discretion grant an extension for good cause shown upon timely written request.

(E)   In no event shall the administrative and regulatory fees payable by the bail bond companies to the fund exceed ten dollars ($10.00) per bond, as required by this subchapter, exclusive of statutory licensure fees elsewhere in this chapter.

(2)(A) Absent an extension the commissioner granted for good cause to a company and in addition to any license suspension or revocation, the commissioner may in his or her discretion order after notice and a hearing a professional bail bond company failing timely to report or pay the regulatory fee to the fund by and through the commissioner shall be liable to the fund for a monetary penalty of one hundred dollars ($100) per day for each day of delinquency.

(B)   The commissioner may pursue any appropriate legal remedies on behalf of the fund to collect any delinquent fees and penalties owed pursuant to this section as special revenues to the fund.

(3)   Upon collection of the regulatory fees and any monetary penalties payable to the fund and assessed under this section, the commissioner shall deposit all fees and penalties directly into the fund as special revenues.

(4)(A) Upon failure of the bail bond company to remit the fees timely, the commissioner may pursue civil legal remedies against the noncomplying bail bond company on behalf of the fund to recover the balance of the fees and any penalties owed.

(B)   In its discretion, the board may also fine, or suspend or revoke the license of, any professional bail bond company failing to remit or pay timely the fees required by this section.

(5)(A) Other than sole proprietors licensed as professional bail bond companies, individual bail bondsmen are exempt from the duty and responsibility of payment of the administrative and regulatory fees to the fund, except that the individual licenses of such individual employees of the professional bail bond company may be suspended or revoked by the commissioner pursuant to the administrative procedures provided in this chapter if the individual licensee fails to comply with his or her duties in proper collection of the bail bond premiums earmarked for later payment to the fund pursuant to this subsection, if he or she converts such moneys to his or her own use, or commits other infractions in regard to collection of such premium amounts.

(B)   In those instances, the violations of the individual may in the commissioner's discretion be attributed to the employing professional bail bond company for good cause shown, and its license may be sanctioned by the commissioner pursuant to the administrative procedures provided in this chapter.

(C)   Further, upon criminal conviction of the individual bondsman for theft of property in connection with fraudulent conversion of those premium amounts due the fund, the board shall revoke the individual's license, and in its discretion fine, or suspend or revoke the license of, the employing professional bail bond company if it assisted the individual in such fraudulent conduct.

(6)(A) For purposes of § 17-19-205 requiring the professional bail bond company's deposit of a letter of credit or certificate of deposit for the faithful performance of its duties, the company's payment of the administrative and regulatory fee as required by this subsection shall be considered to be and shall be a duty of the licensee so as to allow the commissioner to make a claim against the security deposit required in § 17-19-205 on behalf of the fund for the balance of any owed and unpaid administrative and regulatory fees the professional bail bond company still owes to the fund, and the commissioner shall promptly proceed to make claims against such security deposits on behalf of the fund, up to the limit of the company's deposit for any remaining fee balance due, in the manner provided in this subchapter for any claim against the deposit required herein.

(B) Under no circumstances shall such deposits held for the fund, or fees or any moneys deposited into the fund be subject to any levy or assessment of any kind, including forfeiture claims, misconduct claims, or general creditor claims of the bail bond company, subject to garnishment or other creditors' remedies under title 16 of this Code or other provisions of Arkansas law.

(e)(1) In addition to the premiums, compensation, and fees allowed in subsections (a) and (d) of this section, each bail bond company shall charge and collect twenty dollars ($20.00) as a nonrefundable fee for the Arkansas Public Defender Commission.

(2) All fees collected shall be forwarded to the commission for deposit into the Public Defender User Fee Fund.

(3)(A) The commission shall deposit the money collected into the existing account within the State Central Services Fund entitled "Public Defender User Fees".

(B)(i) Three dollars ($3.00) of each fee collected under this section shall be remitted to each county in the state to defray the operating expenses of each county's public defender office.

(ii) The commission shall remit quarterly to each county treasurer the county's portion of the fee collected under this section using the formula for the County Aid Fund under § 19-5-602.

(4) The fees collected by the bail bond companies required under this subsection shall be reported and filed with the commission quarterly.

(5) A notarized annual reconciliation of all fees collected in the preceding calendar year shall be filed by each bail bond company by February 15 on forms provided by the commission.

(6) In addition to the bail or appearance bond premium or compensation allowed under this section and § 17-19-111, each licensed professional bail bond company shall charge and collect a processing fee of five dollars ($5.00) on each bail bond in order to defray the surety's costs incurred by the quarterly and annual reports to the commission and to further defray the surety's costs incurred in the collection of all fees due owing and collected on behalf of the commission.

(7) The commission may pursue any appropriate legal remedy for the collection of any delinquent fees owed under this subsection.

(8) Upon collection of any fees and penalties, the commission shall deposit all

fees and penalties directly into the Public Defender User Fees Fund account within the State Central Services Fund.

History: Acts 1989, No. 417, § 1; 1993, No. 652, § 6; 1995, No. 827, § 6; 1997, No. 1000, §§ 12-14; 2003, No. 1778, § 1; 2005, No. 1956, § 1; 2007, No. 190, § 1; 2007, No. 730, §§ 2, 3.

§ 17-19-302. Collateral — Receipt required

When a licensee accepts collateral, he or she shall give a prenumbered written receipt for it, and this receipt shall give in detail a full account of the collateral received. The licensee may perfect his or her lien on the collateral by any procedure available under the Uniform Commercial Code, § 4-1-101 et seq., or any other procedure provided for by law.

History: Acts 1989, No. 417, § 1; 1997, No. 973, § 9.

§ 17-19-303. Bail bonds — Numbers — Report

(a)   Bail bonds shall be written on numbered forms.

(b)   The Professional Bail Bond Company and Professional Bail Bondsman Licensing Board shall assign numbers for forms to professional bail bond companies and shall prescribe the method of affixing the numbers to the forms.

(c)(1) Each professional bail bond company shall file a bail bond report quarterly with the board.
(2)   The report shall include the following information on each bail bond:
(A)   The assigned number of the bond and current status of the bond, whether pending disposition or exonerated;
(B)   To whom the bond was written;
(C)   The date the bail bond was written;
(D)   The defendant and the charges against the defendant;
(E)   The court;
(F)   The amount of the bail bond; and
(G)   The portion of the bail bond that is secured and the unsecured portion.

History: Acts 1989, No. 417, § 1; 1995, No. 827, § 7.

§ 17-19-304.   Maximum amount of unsecured bond

The maximum amount of unsecured bond commitment allowed for a professional bail bond company shall be determined by the following formulas:

(1)   Not to exceed one hundred thousand dollars ($100,000) for each twenty-five thousand dollars ($25,000) of letters of credit or certificates of deposit filed with the Professional Bail Bond Company and Professional Bail Bondsman Licensing Board by the professional bail bond company; and

(2)   Ten (10) times the net worth of the professional bail bond company as stated on the financial statement filed with the board at the time of licensing or annual license renewal. The financial statements must be prepared in accordance with standards established by the American Institute of Certified Public Accountants.

History: Acts 1989, No. 417, § 1; 1993, No. 1278, § 1; 1995, No. 827, § 7.

§ 17-19-305.   Appearance bond

Upon issuance of the license, a professional bail bondsman shall not issue an appearance bond exceeding the monetary amount for each recognizance which is specified in and authorized by the power of attorney filed with the Professional Bail Bond Company and Professional Bail Bondsman Licensing Board until the board receives a duly executed power of attorney from the professional bail bond company evidencing or authorizing increased monetary limits or amounts for the recognizance.

History: Acts 1989, No. 417, § 1.

§ 17-19-306.   Posting of bondsmen list

(a)(1) The chief law enforcement officers of any facilities having individuals or prisoners in their custody shall post in plain view in the facility housing those individuals or prisoners a list of registered bonding companies.

(2)   The list shall be prepared by the Professional Bail Bond Company and Professional Bail Bondsman Licensing Board and shall contain the names of the professional bail bond companies that are registered with the board for the purpose of being included on the list.

(3)   This registration is for the purpose of being on the phone list in each county only.

(4)(A)   Once a professional bail bond company has registered to be on the phone list, it shall not be necessary for it to register each year.

(B)   The company shall keep its place on the list from year to year unless the company's license has been revoked, canceled, or not renewed.

(5)   The list shall be posted in each municipality of the county.

(b)(1)(A)   Professional bail bond companies shall be included on the list in the order in which they were initially registered with the circuit clerk pursuant to this chapter.

(B)   However, a company with a revoked, canceled, or nonrenewed license shall be removed from the list.

(2)(A)   On or before January 1, 2008, the circuit clerk of each county shall certify the list as it exists on the date of certification and forward the certified list to the board.

(B)   After January 1, 2008, the board shall maintain the list and be responsible for registrations.

(3)(A)   The order of the company names shall not change from year to year.

(B)   However, a company with a revoked, canceled, or nonrenewed license shall be removed from the list.

(c)   The list shall be prepared by the board pursuant to the following specifications:

(1)   The list shall contain three (3) columns that shall be headed as follows:

(A)   Bail bond company;

(B)   Local address; and

(C)   Telephone number;

(2)   Each column shall contain the following information:

(A)   Bail Bond Company. The professional bail bond company name and code number shall be typed in the first column on the left-hand side of the page, with the home office address, city, state, zip code, and home office telephone numbers directly under the company name in the same column. No more than two (2) telephone numbers shall be listed for each company;

(B)   Local Address. The second column shall contain one (1) address for each bail bond company; and

(C)   Telephone Number. The third column shall contain no more than two (2) telephone numbers per company, to be typed directly across the page from the local address, which appears in the second column; and

(3)   A solid line shall be placed between the end of the listing of one company and the beginning of the listing of the next company so that each company is clearly identified.

(d)   The list shall be prepared by the board in the format of the following example:

EXAMPLE

BAIL BOND COMPANY	LOCAL ADDRESS	TELEPHONE #

1. Company Name # AZ
Home Office Address
City, State, Zip
Home Office
Phone Number(s) (2)

555-0000
1-800-666-0000

2. Company Name # ZA
Home Office Address
City, State, Zip
Home Office Phone Number(s) (2)

3. Company Name # DX
Home Office Address
City, State, Zip
Home Office Phone Number(s) (2)

History: Acts 1989, No. 417, § 1; 1993, No. 402, § 1; 2001, No. 1139, § 1; 2007, No. 674, § 2.

§ 17-19-401.   Requirements

(a)   Each person licensed as a professional bail bondsman shall annually complete not less than six (6) hours of continuing education in subjects relating to the authority and responsibilities of a bail bondsman as a condition of renewing his or her license.

(b)   The continuing education shall not include written or oral examinations.

History: Acts 1993, No. 499, § 2; 1999, No. 567, § 4; 2005, No. 1935, § 1.

§ 17-19-402. Establishment of program — Schedule of fees

(a)   The Professional Bail Bond Company and Professional Bail Bondsman Licensing Board shall on an annual basis solicit proposals from education applicants which are approved by the State Board of Private Career Education as education providers, and upon review of the proposals, shall designate an entity or entities to establish an educational program for professional bail bondsmen which will enable bail bondsmen to meet the prelicense and continuing education requirements of § 17-19-212 and 17-19-401 et seq.

(b)(1) The board or its designee shall establish a schedule of fees to be paid by each bail bondsman for the educational training.

(2)   The schedule of fees shall be subject to approval of the board.

History: Acts 1993, No. 499, § 4; 1997, No. 909, § 1.

ARKANSAS COURT RULES

Arkansas Rules Appellate Procedure–Criminal

Rule 6. Bail on appeal

(a)   The appeal bond provided for in this rule shall be filed in the office of the clerk of the court in which the conviction is had, and a copy thereof shall be attached to the bill of exceptions and shall be made a part of the transcript to be filed in the Supreme Court.

(b)(1) When a defendant has been found guilty, pleaded guilty, or pleaded nolo contendere to an offense other than one specified in subsection (b)(2) or (b)(3) of this section, and he is sentenced to serve a term of imprisonment, and he has filed a notice of appeal, the trial court shall not release the defendant on bail or otherwise pending appeal unless it finds:

(A)   By clear and convincing evidence that the defendant is not likely to flee or that there is no substantial risk that the defendant will commit a serious crime, intimidate witnesses, harass or take retaliatory action against any juror, or otherwise interfere with the administration of justice or pose a danger to the safety of any other person; and

(B)   That the appeal is not for the purpose of delay and that it raises a substantial question of law or fact.

(2)   When the defendant has been found guilty, pleaded guilty, or pleaded nolo contendere to capital murder, the trial court shall not release the defendant on bail or otherwise, pending appeal or for any reason.

(3)   When the defendant has been found guilty, pleaded guilty, or pleaded nolo contendere to murder in the first degree, rape, aggravated robbery, or causing a catastrophe, or kidnapping or arson when classified as a Class Y felony, and he has been sentenced to death or imprisonment, the trial court shall not release him on bail or otherwise, pending appeal or for any reason.

(c)(1) If an appeal bond is granted by the trial court, it shall be conditioned on the defendant's surrendering himself to the sheriff of the county in which the trial was held upon the dismissal of the appeal or upon the rendition of final judgment upon the appeal. The trial court may also condition release by imposing restrictions specified in ARCrP 9.3 or other restrictions found reasonably necessary.

(2)   Following the affirmance or reversal of a conviction, or the dismissal of an appeal, the Clerk of the Supreme Court shall immediately make and forward to the clerk of the circuit court of the county in which the defendant was convicted a certified copy of the mandate of the Supreme Court.

(3)   The circuit clerk, upon receipt of a mandate affirming the conviction, shall

immediately file the mandate and notify the sheriff and the bail bondsman or, in appropriate cases, other sureties on the bail bond that the defendant should be surrendered to the sheriff as required by the terms of the bail bond.

(4) If the defendant fails to surrender himself to the sheriff in compliance with the conditions of his bond, the sheriff shall notify the clerk of the circuit court, and the circuit court shall direct that fact to be entered on its records and shall adjudge the bail bond of the defendant, or the money deposited in lieu thereof, to be forfeited.

(5) The defendant having failed to surrender, the circuit clerk shall immediately issue a summons against the sureties on the bail bond requiring them to appear and show cause why judgment should not be rendered against them for the sum specified in the bail bond on account of the forfeiture thereof, which summons shall be made returnable and shall be executed as in civil actions, and the action shall be docketed and shall proceed as an ordinary civil action.

(6) The summons may be served as provided by law in any place in which the sureties may be found, and the service of the summons on the defendant or defendants shall give the court complete jurisdiction of the defendant and cause.

(7) No pleadings on the part of the state shall be required in such cases.

(d) The circuit court in which the defendant was convicted shall retain jurisdiction to hear and decide any motion to revoke the bail of a defendant set at liberty pursuant to this rule, even if the record on appeal has been lodged with the Supreme Court or the Court of Appeals.

(e) If the court in which the defendant was convicted refuses to grant an appeal bond, and an appeal bond shall thereafter be granted by any Justice or Justices of the Supreme Court, the bond shall be conditioned that, upon the dismissal of the appeal or the rendition of the final judgment therein by the Supreme Court, the defendant shall surrender himself as provided in this rule in execution of the judgment.

History: Amended March 27, 1995; adopted and amended July 10, 1995, effective January 1, 1996; amended effective October 21, 1999

Arkansas Rules of Criminal Procedure

Rule 9.1. Release on order to appear or on defendant's own recognizance

(a) At the first appearance the judicial officer may release the defendant on his personal recognizance or upon an order to appear.

(b) Where conditions of release are found necessary, the judicial officer should impose one (1) or more of the following conditions:

(i)   place the defendant under the care of a qualified person or organization agreeing to supervise the defendant and assist him in appearing in court;

(ii)   place the defendant under the supervision of a probation officer or other appropriate public official;

(iii)   impose reasonable restrictions on the activities, movements, associations, and residences of the defendant;

(iv)   release the defendant during working hours but require him to return to custody at specified times; or

(v)   impose any other reasonable restriction to ensure the appearance of the defendant.

Rule 9.2. Release on money bail

(a)   The judicial officer shall set money bail only after he determines that no other conditions will reasonably ensure the appearance of the defendant in court.

(b)   If it is determined that money bail should be set, the judicial officer shall require one (1) of the following:

(i)   the execution of an unsecured bond in an amount specified by the judicial officer, either signed by other persons or not;

(ii)   the execution of an unsecured bond in an amount specified by the judicial officer, accompanied by a deposit of cash or securities equal to ten per cent (10%) of the face amount of the bond. Ninety per cent (90%) of the deposit shall be returned at the conclusion of the proceedings, provided the defendant has not defaulted in the performance of the conditions of the bond; or

(iii)   the execution of a bond secured by the deposit of the full amount in cash, or by other property, or by obligation of qualified sureties.

(c)   In setting the amount of bail the judicial officer should take into account all facts relevant to the risk of wilful nonappearance including:

(i)   the length and character of the defendant's residence in the community;

(ii)   his employment status, history and financial condition;

(iii)   his family ties and relationship;

(iv)   his reputation, character and mental condition;

(v)   his past history of response to legal process;

(vi)   his prior criminal record;

(vii)   the identity of responsible members of the community who vouch for the defendant's reliability;

(viii) the nature of the current charge, the apparent probability of conviction and the likely sentence, in so far as these factors are relevant to the risk of nonappearance;

and

(ix)   any other factors indicating the defendant's roots in the community.

(d)   Nothing in this rule shall be construed to prohibit a judicial officer from permitting a defendant charged with an offense other than a felony from posting a specified sum of money which may be forfeited or applied to a fine and costs in lieu of any court appearance.

(e)   An appearance bond and any security deposit required as a condition of release pursuant to subsection (b) of this rule shall serve to guarantee all subsequent appearances of a defendant on the same charge or on other charges arising out of the same conduct before any court, including appearances relating to appeals and upon remand. If the defendant is required to appear before a court other than the one ordering release, the order of release together with the appearance bond and any security or deposit shall be transmitted to the court before which the defendant is required to appear. This subsection shall not be construed to prevent a judicial officer from:

(i)   decreasing the amount of bond, security or deposit required by another judicial officer; or

(ii)   upon making written findings that factors exist increasing the risk of wilful nonappearance, increasing the amount of bond, security, or deposit required by another judicial officer.

Upon an increase in the amount of bond or security, a surety may surrender defendant.

Rule 9.3. Prohibition of wrongful acts pending trial

If it appears that there exists a danger that the defendant will commit a serious crime or will seek to intimidate witnesses, or will otherwise unlawfully interfere with the orderly administration of justice, the judicial officer, upon the release of the defendant, may enter an order:

(a)   prohibiting the defendant from approaching or communicating with particular persons or classes of persons, except that no such order shall be deemed to prohibit any lawful and ethical activity of defendant's counsel;

(b)   prohibiting the defendant from going to certain described geographical areas or premises;

(c)   prohibiting the defendant from possessing any dangerous weapon, or engaging in certain described activities or indulging in intoxicating liquors or in certain drugs;

(d)   requiring the defendant to report regularly to and remain under the supervision of an officer of the court.

PART II.
SUMMARY OF CASE LAW ON RIGHT TO PURSUE A FUGITIVE

State v. Mathis, 349 N.C. 503, 509 S.E. 2d 155 (1998)
[partially redacted]

[Defendants were employees of a bail bondsman who were instructed to recapture a fugitive who lived with his mother. They were convicted of breaking and entering and appealed. The North Carolina Court of Appeals held in an unpublished opinion that the common law right of bondsmen to recapture was a defense to the charge denied them at trial. The state sought review by the state Supreme Court.]

While defendant Mathis held the storm door, defendant Willamson entered the house. At this point, defendant Mathis released the storm door and also entered the house. They were followed by Mrs. Nelson, [the fugitive's mother,] who then called the police. Defendant Williamson proceeded to search the rooms in the house but did not enter a locked front bedroom because Mr. Nelson told him a baby was asleep inside.

After arriving on the scene, the police asked defendants to step outside and told them that they would notify them when the arrest was made. At 2:00 a.m., having not received the call, defendants went back to Mr. Tankersley's residence. After they saw the white Mazda in the driveway, defendants flagged down a police officer who helped them take Mr. Tankersley into custody.

At the conclusion of the evidence, the trial court conducted a jury charge conference. At that time, defendants requested that the trial court include in its final instructions to the jury instructions defining the authority of bail bondsmen to break and enter the home of a principal and to use such force as reasonably necessary to apprehend him. The trial court denied this request.

At the conclusion of the trial court's final instructions to the jury, the trial court asked if the State or defendants wished to have any additional instructions given. Defendants again requested that appropriate instructions be given regarding the authority of bail bondsmen and made specific requests that the trial court read portions of certain opinions of this Court defining that authority as it related to the evidence presented at trial. The trial court again denied defendants' requests. Defendants were found guilty of all charges.

Defendants appealed to the North Carolina Court of Appeals. In a unanimous opinion, the Court of Appeals reversed the convictions and remanded defendants' cases for a new trial, concluding that the trial court had erred "by failing to instruct the jury on the common law and statutory authority of bail bonds-men to break and enter a principal's home to accomplish a lawful arrest." State v. Mathis, 126 N.C. App. 688, 693, 486 S.E.2d 475, 478 (1997). The Court of Appeals also concluded that the jury should have been instructed regarding the privilege of bail bondsmen to use reasonable force and the prohibition against their use of excessive force when apprehending their principal.

This Court granted the State's petition for certiorari on 5 February 1998. In analyzing the authority granted bail bondsmen, two issues are before us: (1) whether a bail bondsman may forcibly enter his principal's residence to search for and seize him; and (2) whether, in the process of gaining entry, a bail bondsman may overcome the resistance of a third party. We conclude that bail bondsmen have both such powers under the common law. Therefore, we answer both of these questions in the affirmative.

We begin our discussion with a brief overview of the history of the American system of bail,[1] which is rooted in the English common law. Jonathan Drimmer, *When Man Hunts Man: The Rights and Duties of Bounty Hunters in the American Criminal Justice System,* 33 Hous. L. Rev. 731, 744 (1996) [hereinafter *When Man Hunts Man*]. Release on bail pending trial developed from "an ancient and extremely vigorous form of suretyship or hostageship, which rendered the surety liable to suffer the punishment that was hanging over the head of the released prisoner." 2 Sir Frederick Pollack & Frederic William Maitland, The History of English Law 589 (2d ed. 1959). The surety was, in effect, "bound body for body" with the principal. Id. at 590.

The now-common practice of allowing the surety to pay a sum of money should the accused not appear for trial was first utilized in the early thirteenth century.[2] By releasing the prisoner into the custody of the surety, not only was the return of the prisoner assured, but also, and importantly, his release strengthened the presumption of innocence fundamental to our system of justice. *Stack v. Boyle,* 342 U.S. 1, 4, 96 L. Ed. 3, 6 (1951). Freedom of the accused protected him from the punishment of pretrial detention and also improved his opportunity to prepare a defense. Id. The release of the prisoner has always been considered a form of continued detention, and the common law viewed the surety's custody as a single, continuous event. "'A man's bail are looked upon as his jailers of his own choosing, and the person bailed is, in the eye of the law, for many purposes, esteemed to be as much in the prison of the court by which he is bailed, as if he were in the actual custody of the proper jailer.'" Annotation, Surrender of Principal by Sureties on Bail Bond, 3 A.L.R. 180, 183 (1919) (quoting II William Hawkins, Pleas of the Crown 138, 138-39 (8th ed. 1824)) (emphasis added).

Similarly, no distinction was made between a law enforcement officer's recapture of an escaped prisoner and a surety's apprehension of his principal; neither was considered an original taking. *Commonwealth v. Brickett,* 25 Mass. (8 Pick.) 138, 141 (1829). The surety was granted the same rights and powers as a sheriff capturing an escaped prisoner and returning him to the proper authorities. Because the principal was never out of the "custody" of the surety, the surety could take him at any time, "when and where he pleases." *Read v. Case,* 4 Conn. 166, 170 (1822).

The United States Constitution recognized the need for bail in our system of justice by requiring that "[e]xcessive bail shall not be required." U.S. Const. amend. VIII. In doing so, the English common law system of bail was adopted. However, due to rapid urbanization and the weakening of close community ties which resulted, by the mid-nineteenth century the personal-surety system of bail utilized for centuries was no longer practical, and the modern-day system of relying on commercial bondsmen[3] evolved. *When*

---

[1] The popular meaning of "bail" is the security given for the appearance of the accused to obtain his release from prison. The person who posts the required amount of bail is generally called the "surety" and in earlier cases simply "bail." The "principal" is the person who has been arrested and is released on bond pending his scheduled court appearance. 8A Am. Jur. 2d Bail & Recognizance § 1 (1997).

[2] In earlier times, the surety was typically an acquaintance of the accused, a property owner, and a reputable member of the community. If the principal failed to appear at trial, the surety would quite often have to forfeit his real property. *When Man Hunts Man,* 33 Hous. L. Rev. at 745.

[3] The bail procedure operates as follows: A relative or friend will contact a bail bondsman, who decides on the basis of the accused's background, criminal record, and community ties whether he is a good risk. If the bondsman decides he will write the bond, he charges a fee, typically ten percent of the full bail amount paid, and presents the court with a bail bond securing release of the defendant, or "principal." If the principal fails to appear for trial as scheduled, the bondsman is responsible for the entire

Man Hunts Man, 33 Hous. L. Rev. at 749. Today's commercial bondsmen have retained the same broad common law powers sureties have always enjoyed regarding the custody, control, and recapture of the principal.

In the most often quoted case in this area of the law, *Taylor v. Taintor,* 83 U.S. 366, 21 L. Ed. 287 (1872), the United States Supreme Court defined the rights and powers of sureties and bail bondsmen at common law:

> When bail is given, the principal is regarded as delivered to the custody of his sureties. Their dominion is a continuation of the original imprisonment. Whenever they choose to do so, they may seize him and deliver him up in their discharge, and if that cannot be done at once, they may imprison him until it can be done. They may exercise their rights in person or by agent. They may pursue him into another State, may arrest him on the Sabbath, and if necessary, may break and enter his house for that purpose. The seizure is not made by virtue of new process. None is needed. It is likened to the rearrest by the sheriff of an escaping prisoner. In 6 Modern [231], it is said: "The bail have their principal on a string, and may pull the string whenever they please and render him in their discharge."

Id. at 371-72, 21 L. Ed. at 290. This decision established the law of the land to be applied in federal courts. *In re Von Der Ahe,* 85 F. 959, 962 (W.D. Pa. 1898).

The comprehensive powers of the bondsman recognized in Taintor are based on the underlying source of the bondsman's authority to recapture the principal which derives from the contractual relationship between the surety and the principal. Essentially, the bond agreement provides that the surety post the bail, and in return, the principal agrees that the surety can retake him at any time, even before forfeiture of the bond. By entering into the contract, not only does the principal voluntarily consent to be committed to the custody of the surety, but under common law, he also implicitly agrees that the surety or the surety's agent may break and enter his home and use reasonable force in apprehending him. Id. at 960. Further, the contract establishes the surety's and bondsman's right of recapture as private in nature, with the understanding that the government will not interfere. *Reese v. United States,* 76 U.S. 13, 22, 19 L. Ed. 541, 544 (1869). Thus, this common law right of recapture established that the seizure of the principal by the surety is technically not an "arrest" at all and may be accomplished without process of law.

We think it important to note here that while most statutory and decisional authorities use the term "arrest" when referring to the recapture of the principal, in this area of the law, that term is not used in the traditional way to mean to "deprive another of his liberty" or "to take custody of." Since the principal is always in the "custody" of the surety, his apprehension by the surety or his agent is merely a "continuation of the original imprisonment." The term "arrest" in the context involved here is meant to convey an "apprehension," "seizure," or "recapture." As the court in *Von Der Ahe* stated in holding that the private contract between the principal and the surety implicitly authorized the surety to seize the principal at any time,

> there is a fundamental difference between the right of arrest by bail and arrest under warrant where such right to arrest is based upon a court process .... The latter right depends upon the process of the court .... The former arrest ... is based upon the relationship which the parties have established between themselves ....

---

financial obligation. Michael Goldstein, *The Hunters and the Hunted: Rights and Liabilities of Bailbondsmen,* 6 Fordham Urb. L.J. 333, 333 n.2 (1978).

Von Der Ahe, 85 F. at 960; see *Fitzpatrick v. Williams,* 46 F.2d 40, 40 (5th Cir. 1931) ("The right of the surety to recapture his principal is not a matter of criminal procedure, but arises from the private undertaking implied in the furnishing of the bail bond. It is not the right of the state but of the surety."); *Nicolls v. Ingersoll,* 7 Johns. 145, 154 (N.Y. 1810) ("[T]his shows that the jurisdiction of the court in no way controls the authority of the bail; and as little can the jurisdiction of the State affect this right, as between the bail and his principal."); see also *State v. Nugent,* 199 Conn. 537, 508 A.2d 728 (1986); *State v. Perry,* 50 N.C. App. 540, 274 S.E.2d 261, appeal dismissed, 302 N.C. 632, 280 S.E.2d 446 (1981). Absent the involvement of the State, the constitutional protections of due process are not implicated.

It has long been settled common law that the surety may use reasonable force to apprehend the principal and may even forcibly enter the principal's residence. "His dwelling is no longer his castle as against the right of the sureties, but may be entered at any time of day or night, and on a Sunday as well as on a week day." *United States v. Keiver,* 56 F. 422, 426 (W.D. Wis. 1893); see also *Brickett,* 25 Mass. (8 Pick.) at 140 ("If the door should not be opened on demand at midnight, the bail may break it down, and take the principal from his bed, if that measure should be necessary ....."); *Nicolls,* 7 Johns. at 155 (the bail is entitled to break the outer door of a dwelling to enter the premises where the principal is). Since the nineteenth century, the common law principles granting sureties and their agents power and authority have been modified very little, if at all. Courts throughout the country have upheld the decisions of the earlier cases, confirming the role of the bondsman in the pretrial process. Numerous cases have reemphasized that the surety and his agents have a right to arrest the principal without a warrant, pursue him across state lines, return him to the home state without extradition proceedings, and use other means necessary to achieve the goal of apprehending the principal. E.g., *Fitzpatrick,* 46 F.2d at 41; *Smith v. Rosenbaum,* 333 F. Supp. 35, 39 (E.D. Pa. 1971), aff'd, 460 F.2d 1019 (3d Cir. 1972); *Curtis v. Peerless Ins. Co.,* 299 F. Supp. 429, 435 (D. Minn. 1969); *Thomas v. Miller,* 282 F. Supp. 571, 573 (E.D. Tenn. 1968); *McCaleb v. Peerless Ins. Co.,* 250 F. Supp. 512, 515 (D. Neb. 1965).

We turn now to an analysis of the applicable law of North Carolina.

> [T]he "common law" to be applied in North Carolina is the common law of England to the extent it was in force and use within this State at the time of the Declaration of Independence; is not otherwise contrary to the independence of this State or the form of government established therefor; and is not abrogated, repealed, or obsolete. N.C.G.S. § 4-1.

Gwathmey v. State ex rel. Dep't of Env't, Health & Natural Resources, 342 N.C. 287, 296, 464 S.E.2d 674, 679 (1995). The common law of North Carolina has always recognized the sweeping powers of sureties, or bail bondsmen who act as their agents, to apprehend the principal and use whatever force is reasonably necessary in the process. *State v. Lingerfelt,* 109 N.C. 775, 14 S.E. 75 (1891). "At common law, when bail was given, and the principal relieved from the custody of the law, he was regarded, not as freed entirely, but as transferred to the friendly custody of his bail. They had a dominion over him, and it was their right at any time to arrest and surrender him again to the custody of the law, in discharge of their obligation." *State v. Schenck,* 138 N.C. 560, 561, 49 S.E. 917, 917-18 (1905). "Persons who become bail are favored by the law, and the powers given the bail over his principal are given to enable him more easily to perform the onerous duties and obligations which he has voluntarily assumed." *Pickelsimer v. Glazener,* 173 N.C. 630, 640, 92 S.E. 700, 705 (1917).

We also note that the authority of the surety, or a bondsman acting as his agent, to apprehend and surrender the principal in accord with the common law principles set out above also finds support in statutory authority:

> For the purposes of surrendering the defendant, the surety may arrest him before the forfeiture of the undertaking, or by his written authority endorsed on a certified copy of

the undertaking, may request any judicial officer to order arrest of the defendant.

N.C.G.S. § 58-71-30 (1994).

(a) A surety may surrender his principal to the sheriff of the county in which the principal is bonded to appear or to the sheriff where the defendant was bonded. A surety may arrest his principal for the purpose of returning him to the sheriff. Upon surrender of the principal the sheriff must provide a receipt to the surety, a copy of which must be filed with the clerk.

N.C.G.S. § 15A-540 (1997). This statutory right of arrest granted the surety does not change -- but simply codifies a part of -- the common law powers of sureties that have always been recognized in our state. *State v. Perry,* 50 N.C. App. 540, 274 S.E.2d 261 (decided under former N.C.G.S. § 85C-7). The arrest provisions of N.C.G.S. § 58-71-30 do not create a law enforcement officer in the person of the bail bondsman. Id. at 542, 274 S.E.2d at 262. "Neither do we conclude that the bondsman's right to request that a judicial officer order the arrest of a defendant creates a law enforcement officer in the person of the bail bondsman." Id. Interestingly, N.C.G.S. § 58-71-105 prohibits law enforcement officers from becoming sureties on a bail bond.

While we acknowledge that the contract between the surety and the principal authorizes the surety to exercise certain powers as to the principal, we do not find that this contractual authority can be extended to cases where a surety is seeking the principal in the home of a third party where the principal does not reside. In those cases the surety must first have the consent of the homeowner to enter the premises and conduct a search. See *State v. Tapia,* 468 N.W.2d 342 (Minn. Ct. App. 1991).

At least one court appears to have indicated that a surety may enter the home of a third party where the principal does not reside even without consent of the owner if (1) the surety identifies himself and makes his intention known, (2) the surety actually sees the principal in the house, and (3) the surety acts in a reasonable manner in gaining entry. *Livingston v. Browder,* 51 Ala. App. 366, 370, 285 So. 2d 923, 927 (1973). We do not agree with this analysis. The right of the surety to enter the residence of his principal and to seize him arises as a matter of contract from the bond agreement which carries with it the principal's implied consent that the surety may seize him at any time and may use such force as is reasonably necessary to enter his residence at any time in order to do so. The principal has no authority to authorize the surety, by contract or otherwise, to enter the residence of a third party in which the principal does not himself reside. Therefore, the surety obtains no such power by virtue of the bond agreement.

When the principal himself resides in the home of a third party, however, a different rule applies. There is "no difference between a house of which [the principal] is solely possessed, and a house in which he resides by the consent of another." *Sheers v. Brooks,* 126 Eng. Rep. 463, 464 (1792); see also *Nicolls,* 7 Johns. at 155. Bond agreements giving, as a matter of law, the principal's consent for the sureties or their agents to break and enter his residence authorize them to enter even when the principal resides there with others. *Nicolls;* see *Mease v. State,* 165 Ga. App. 746, 302 S.E.2d 429 (1983).

This brings us to the final question of whether sureties or their agents may lawfully overcome the resistance of a third party who is impeding their apprehension of the principal. Although we have found no North Carolina case directly on point, it is generally recognized that

[w]here the third person knowingly causes the arrestor to believe that he or she is intentionally impeding the privileged arrest or recapture of a suspect or is attempting to rescue or assist the suspect in resisting arrest or escaping therefrom, the arrestor is privileged to use such force against the third person as he or she would be privileged to use against one

who resisted or attempted escape.

5 Am. Jur. 2d Arrest § 116 (1995). Therefore, we conclude that sureties or their agents may use such force as is reasonably necessary to overcome the resistance of a third party who attempts to impede their privileged capture of their principal. But they may use only such force as is reasonably necessary under the circumstances to accomplish the arrest.

. . .

In the present case, evidence tended to show that defendants were licensed bail bondsmen employed by Marie's Bail Bonding, which issued Mr. Tankersley's bond. Mr. Tankersley testified that 8 Willowbrook Drive was his residence, and that is where he was later arrested. Furthermore, Mrs. Nelson testified that he resided in the house with her. Ms. Noto and Ms. McKnight also testified that he lived at the house. This was sufficient evidence to permit a properly instructed jury to find that the house was, in fact, Mr. Tankersley's residence.

As we have explained in detail above, the surety or a bondsman acting as his agent has the authority and the contractual right to break and enter the principal's residence and to use the force reasonably necessary to apprehend him. Therefore, a properly instructed jury could find that when Mr. Tankersley failed to appear in court according to the terms of his bail bond, defendants were exercising their common law rights as bondsmen to break and enter his residence at 8 Willowbrook Drive to seize him.

Again, we stress that although evidence suggested that Mrs. Nelson was the owner of the home, this alone would not create a case of violation of a third party's privacy rights. Evidence tended to show that Mr. Tankersley also was a resident there. Even a warrantless search by a police officer may be consented to by a common resident or cotenant who possesses common authority or other sufficient relationship to the premises, regardless of the fact that the property may contain evidence incriminating another person. 68 Am. Jur. 2d Searches and Seizures § 92 (1993). A surety enters pursuant to the consent of his principal, which is valid if the principal is a common resident in the premises. See *Mease v. State,* 165 Ga. App. 746, 302 S.E.2d 429 (1983) (Two bondsmen went looking for their principal at the house where she lived with someone else. After being told by the other occupant of the house that she was not there, and without consent, the bondsmen entered the residence and searched for the principal. The defendants in that case were found not guilty of criminal trespass because the court found that the evidence did not support a finding that they had entered the house for an "unlawful purpose."). Here, there was evidence that 8 Willowbrook Drive was Mr. Tankersley's residence. Therefore, a properly instructed jury could find that defendants had the authority and a legitimate right to enter and to search for Mr. Tankersley inside the house at 8 Willowbrook Drive.

Furthermore, evidence was introduced from which a jury could find that defendants had a reasonable belief that Mr. Tankersley was inside his residence. Evidence tended to show that defendants were notified by another bondsman watching the residence that Mr. Tankersley had come home. Upon arriving at the house, defendants noticed the white Mazda parked in the driveway; the Mazda had not been there earlier, and Mr. Tankersley had indicated on the bond application that it was the car he drove. Mrs. Nelson made quite an effort to keep defendants out of the house. There was also evidence of a locked bedroom to which defendants were denied access because they were told a sleeping baby was inside. From such evidence, a jury could find that defendants were within the limits of their powers as bondsmen in conducting a search of the residence.

As to the reasonableness of defendant Mathis' actions, we note that upon encountering Mrs. Nelson in the residence of the principal, Mathis was met with some resistance. Evidence tended to show that when he identified himself and stated his intentions, Mrs. Nelson denied him entry and blocked the door.

According to the testimony of defendant Mathis, she began striking him about the chest and shoulders. Pushing the door against her, Mathis forced his way in. Mrs. Nelson testified that she was not injured.

We are not suggesting that there are no limits to a bondsman's powers. However, a jury could find from such evidence that the bondsmen here had a reasonable belief that Mr. Tankersley was in his residence, that Mrs. Nelson was interfering with the arrest, and that the bondsmen were justified in using the force necessary to enter and seize Mr. Tankersley.

For the foregoing reasons, we conclude that the trial court should have instructed the jury on the common law and statutory authority of bail bondsmen. The decision of the Court of Appeals to reverse the judgment of the Superior Court and remand for a new trial due to the trial court's failure to give such instructions is therefore affirmed.

AFFIRMED.

[concurring and dissenting opinions omitted]

———————

Accord: *State v. Kole,* 92 Ohio St. 3d 303, 750 NE 2d 148 (2001) (defense counsel was ineffective for not submitting a jury instruction on a bail bondsman's privilege to enter the home of the principal to take him into custody).

Entering an innocent third party's home is likely a burglary. *State v. McFarland,* 598 NW 2d 318 (Iowa Ct. App. 1999); *State v. Burhans,* 277 Kan. 858, 89 P.3d 629 (2004); *State v. Tapia,* 468 N.W.2d 342 (Minn. Ct. App. 1991); *State v. Lopez,* 105 N.M. 538, 734 P.2d 778 (Ct. App. 1986)

Texas holds that *Taylor v. Tainter* is replaced by statute, and the Uniform Criminal Extradition Act applies to interstate removals. *Green v. State,* 829 S.W.2d 222 (Tex. Crim. App. 1992).

PART III.

RULES AND REGULATIONS
OF THE ARKANSAS BAIL BOND BOARD

Rule and Regulation 1, Regulation of Bail Bond Business. 63

Appendices. 93

Rule and Regulation 2. Regulation of the Education Program. 107

RULE AND REGULATION 1
REGULATION OF BAIL BOND BUSINESS

1.	Purpose.	66
2.	Authority.	66
3.	Effective Date and Applicability.	66
4.	Definitions.	66
5.	Bail Bond Form.	68
6.	Qualifying Power of Attorney Form.	68
7.	Regular Power of Attorney Form.	69
8.	Company Codes.	69
9.	Quarterly Reports.	70
10.	Secured Bail Bonds.	70
11.	Unsecured Bond Commitment; Penalties.	71
12.	Clean Irrevocable Letter of Credit.	72
13.	Certificate of Deposit.	72
14.	Certificate of Deposit and Clean Irrevocable Letter of Credit; Release.	72
15.	Licenses.	73
16.	License Required.	74
17.	Transfer of Bondsman License.	75
18.	License Renewal, Continuing Education Required.	77
19.	License Denial – Company.	78
20.	License Denial – Bondsman.	78
21.	Financial Statements; Guidelines	79
22.	Collateral; Fiduciary Relationship.	80
23.	Return of Excess Collateral on Forfeiture; Expenses.	81
24.	Refund of Premium.	81
25.	Allowable Charges.	81
26.	Forfeitures; Misrepresentations.	82
27.	Unpaid Forfeitures and Misconduct; License Sanctions.	82
28.	Bail Bond Complaint Form and Procedures.	83
29.	Complaints, Cooperation Required.	83
30.	Hearing Officer.	84
31.	Hearings, Revocation or Suspension of License.	84
32.	Gifts Prohibited.	86
33.	Notice of Change of Address.	86
34.	Written Statement of Bail Transaction; Contents.	87
35.	Examinations.	87
36.	Record Retention.	88
37.	Company Appointment.	88
38.	Advertising.	88
39.	Apprehension of Defendants.	89

40.	Compliance with Posted Rules of Jails	90
41.	Severability	91

Appendix A – Bail Bond Form	93
Appendix B – Affidavit of Sole Proprietorship	94
Appendix C – Statement of Bail and Payment Received	95
Appendix D – Qualifying Power of Attorney	96
Appendix E – Quarterly Report Form	97
Appendix F – Clean Irrevocable Letter of Credit	99
Appendix G – Bail Bond Complaint Form	102
Appendix H – Advertising Examples	104
Appendix I – Authorization by Surety to Arrest Defendant on Bail Bond	105
Appendix J – Collateral Receipt (Example)	106

SECTION 1.   PURPOSE

The purpose of this Rule and Regulation ("rule") is to set specific requirements that should be followed by professional bail bond companies and professional bail bondsman engaged in the bail bond business in this State, pursuant to Act 417 of 1989, codified as Ark. Code Ann. Section 17-19-101 et seq., as amended.

SECTION 2.   AUTHORITY

This rule is issued pursuant to the authority vested in the Board under Ark. Code Ann. Sections 25-15-201, et seq., 17-19-106 and all other applicable provisions of Arkansas law.

SECTION 3.   EFFECTIVE DATE AND APPLICABILITY

This rule shall be effective October 1, 2005 and shall be applicable to all qualified professional bail bond companies and their licensees and all applicants for a professional bail bond company or individual bail bondsman license.

SECTION 4.   DEFINITIONS

The following definitions as used in this rule shall have the following meaning:

A.   "Board" shall mean the Arkansas Professional Bail Bond Company and Professional Bail Bondsman Licensing Board/Arkansas Professional Bail Bondsman Licensing Board;

Â.   "Director" shall mean the Executive Director of the Board;

C.   "Company" shall mean a professional bail bond company as defined by Ark. Code Ann. Section 17-19-101(7);

D.   "Bail bondsman" shall mean a professional bail bondsman as defined by Ark. Code Ann. Section 17-19-101(6);

E.   "Premium" shall mean the money paid to a bail bondsman or professional bail bond company for release of an arrestee;

F.   "Arrestee" shall mean any person actually detained or subject to detention in custody whose release may lawfully be effected by bail;

G.   "Licensee" shall mean a professional bail bond company or a professional bail bondsman;

H.   "Bail bond" shall mean a bond for a specified monetary amount executed by the defendant or principal and a qualified licensee which is issued to a court, magistrate, or authorized officer as security for the subsequent appearance of the defendant upon his release from actual custody pending the appearance;

I.   "Jail" shall mean any police station, sheriff's office or other place where persons in the custody of the law are detained;

J.   "Principal" shall mean the person(s) paying the bail bond premium and/or giving the collateral;

K.   "Surety" shall mean the person/company responsible for the appearance of the defendant in court;

L.   "Private Investigator" shall mean an Arkansas licensed private investigator as defined by Ark. Code. Ann. § 17-40-102(9);

M.   "Bail Enforcement Agent/Bounty Hunter" shall mean a person who is offered or given any compensation by a bail bond company/ bail bondsman or surety in exchange for assisting the bail bondsman or surety in apprehending or surrendering any defendant. This does not preclude the right of bail bondsman or sureties to hire counsel or to ask assistance of law enforcement officers.

N. "Stacking" shall mean executing more than one bond to avoid exceeding a bail bondsman's current Qualifying Power of Attorney.

O. "Direct Supervision" means the person is in the physical presence of, and acting pursuant to instructions from, an Arkansas licensed bail bondsman.

SECTION 5.   BAIL BOND FORM

Every bail bond issued by a professional bail bond company or its licensee(s) shall conform exactly to the forms prescribed in Appendices "A" and "B", shall have attached to it a "Statement of Bail and Payment Received" as prescribed in Appendix "C" and shall be preprinted with sequential numbers.

SECTION 6.   QUALIFYING POWER OF ATTORNEY FORM

A. Each company, upon either an initial or renewal application for a company license, must submit to this Board a Qualifying Power of Attorney from the company, specifying the authority limits of each of its licensees.

B. A new Qualifying Power of Attorney must be submitted to this Board immediately for any increases, decreases or other changes made between licensing periods.

C. The original Qualifying Power of Attorney increase signed by the bail bondsman/attorney-in-fact, must be received by the Board prior to a bail bondsman initiating a bond for the increased amount.

D. Qualifying Power of Attorney increases shall not be submitted for the purpose of allowing a bail bondsman to write a bond that violates his/her existing Qualifying Power of Attorney or with the intent of reversing the increase subsequent to the bond being written.

E.   The Qualifying Power of Attorney shall be executed in the form prescribed in Appendix "D" of this rule.

F.   All licensed bail bondsmen shall, at any time they are writing bonds, carry a current copy of their Qualifying Power of Attorney that is on file with the Arkansas Professional Bail Bond Licensing Board.

G.   Only one power of attorney per bond, not exceeding the bail bondsman's Qualifying Power of Attorney, is allowed, unless a court has separated the charges and amounts of bonds. Powers of attorney shall not be stacked.

H.   Those companies operating as sole proprietorships shall not be required to execute and file a Qualifying Power of Attorney form unless such company has licensees other than the sole proprietor.

SECTION 7. REGULAR POWER OF ATTORNEY FORM

A.   Every bond executed by a bail bondsman shall include a numbered power of attorney indicating a valid appointment from a professional bail bond company and referring to that company.

B.   The power of attorney shall be in the form prescribed in Appendix "A" of this rule and shall have "Item 2" preprinted.

C.   A sole proprietor of a company shall include on bonds he executes an affidavit of sole proprietorship in the form prescribed by Appendix "B" of this rule.

SECTION 8. COMPANY CODES

A.   Upon issuance of a license to a professional bail bond company, the Board shall assign an alpha code that will be exclusive to that company. For each individual licensee of that company, the Board will assign a consecutive numerical code.

B.   Company codes and individual bond numbers shall be preprinted sequentially in the upper right hand corner of all bail bonds, powers of attorney, statements of bail and premium receipts executed by the licensee. The bail bondsman's code may be written in ink between the company code and the bond number.

SECTION 9. QUARTERLY REPORTS

A. Every company shall file with the Board a quarterly report as required by Ark. Code Ann. Section 17-19-303(c). The report shall be made in the form as prescribed in Appendix "E" of this rule. The form shall be either typed or computer generated. Bonds shall be listed in sequential number order.

B. The quarterly report due dates are as follows:

Period Covered	Due Date
July 1 - September 30	October 15
October 1 - December 31	January 15
January 1 - March 31	April 15
April 1 - June 30	July 15

C. Quarterly reports must be received by the Board on the above referenced due dates by 4:30 p.m.

D. Companies may request an extension of time for filing a Quarterly Report by submitting a written request to the Director. Such request must be received and approved in advance of the due date, and must be for good cause shown.

E. If the quarterly report is not received as required by Subsection "C" above and no extension has been granted pursuant to Subsection "D" above, the offending company will be immediately suspended.

F. A penalty of One Hundred Dollars ($100.00) per day will be assessed until the report is received, beginning the day after the report is due.

G. The company license will be reinstated upon the payment of said penalty and the signing of a consent order.

SECTION 10. SECURED BAIL BONDS

A. A "secured" bail bond is one that is secured by a grant of an interest in identifiable, tangible property.

B. A promissory note, whether or not co-signed, will not be considered security.

C. A bail bond is only secured up to an amount equal to the fair market value of the interest granted in tangible property.

D.   If the amount of the bond exceeds the value of the security, that amount so exceeding the value of the security shall be considered unsecured.

E.   Signatures of principals and/or indemnifiers that are not given in the presence of the bail bondsman shall be notarized.

SECTION 11. UNSECURED BOND COMMITMENT; PENALTIES

A.   The amount of unsecured bond commitments that a bail bond company can have outstanding at any given time will be determined by the Board or its Designee pursuant to Ark. Code Ann. Section 17-19-304.

B.   Companies using the "ten (10) times" formula pursuant to Ark. Code Ann. Section 17-19-304(2) must submit financial statements prepared in accordance with standards for audits or reviews as established by the American Institute of Certified Public Accountants.

C.   If a professional bail bond company exceeds the unsecured bond commitment amount prescribed by Ark. Code Ann. Section 17-19-304, such company will have twenty (20) days from the date of written notice from the Board to bring its unsecured bond commitment into compliance with Code requirements. However, no unsecured bonds shall be written while such company is out of compliance.

D.   Any company on notice that it is out of compliance shall submit proof within twenty (20) days that it has rectified the violation by the posting of an additional certificate of deposit or clean irrevocable letter of credit for an additional amount.

E.   The license of any company that fails to cure its violations of Ark. Code Ann. Section 17-19-304 may be suspended by order of the Board, and a hearing to show cause why the license should not be revoked shall be held within ten (10) days of the suspension. If, after hearing, the Board finds that an un-rectified violation exists, it may revoke the license of the offending company.

SECTION 12. CLEAN IRREVOCABLE LETTER OF CREDIT

A.	Every company posting a clean irrevocable letter of credit with the Board pursuant to Ark. Code Ann. Section 17-19-205(a)(2)(A) shall post such letter using the form approved by the Board and contained in Appendix "F" of this rule. Copies of the clean irrevocable letter of credit may be obtained from the Board.

B.	Substituted forms from financial institutions are not acceptable.

C.	No letter of credit shall be subject to termination or cancellation by either party in less than sixty (60) days after the giving of written notice thereof to the other parties and the Board. Notice of termination or cancellation to the Board shall be by certified mail, return receipt requested.

D.	No termination or cancellation shall affect the liability of the surety or sureties on a bond incurred prior to the effective date of termination or cancellation.

SECTION 13. CERTIFICATES OF DEPOSIT

A.	Any certificate of deposit filed with the Board pursuant to Ark. Code Ann. Section 17-19-205(a)(1) shall be a certificate of deposit issued by an Arkansas or federally chartered bank located in Arkansas.

B.	No certificate of deposit shall be subject to termination or cancellation by either party in less than sixty (60) days after the giving of written notice thereof to the other parties and the Board. Notice of termination or cancellation to the Board shall be by certified mail, return receipt requested.

C.	No termination or cancellation shall affect the liability of the surety or sureties on a bond incurred prior to the effective date of termination or cancellation.

## SECTION 14.	CERTIFICATE OF DEPOSIT AND CLEAN IRREVOCABLE LETTER OF CREDIT; RELEASE

Any company desiring the release of a certificate of deposit or clean irrevocable letter of credit that has been filed with the Board shall comply with either of the following requirements:

A.   A company seeking release of a certificate of deposit or a clean irrevocable letter of credit may file with the Board a replacement security in an amount equal to or greater than the amount of the security for which release is sought, and the replacement security must be specifically retroactive to the date the original security was issued.

B.   If a company wishes to procure the release of a clean irrevocable letter of credit or of a certificate of deposit, it must present a statement in writing from each court of each county in which the company was engaged in business to write bail bonds, stating that the company has satisfied all its outstanding liabilities, both actual and potential; that no outstanding forfeitures against the company remain; that all bail bonds which were issued by the company have been discharged; and that all civil judgments as to forfeitures on bonds issued by the licensee have been paid in full.

SECTION 15.   LICENSES

A.   At least one owner/officer/partner must be a licensed bail bondsman licensed in two of the preceding three years.

B.   All company owners/officers/directors/stockholders/partners will be required to apply to the Identification Bureau of the Department of Arkansas State Police for a state and nationwide criminal records check to be conducted by the Federal Bureau of Investigation. The criminal records checks will be required for any company licensee regardless of whether the owner/applicant is a licensed Arkansas bail bondsman.

C.   Changes in ownership or changes to the corporate structure of any Arkansas licensed bail bond company shall be transmitted to the Board via a completed bail bond company application indicating the change. Criminal record checks will be submitted for those owners/officers/ directors/stockholders/partners not previously listed.

D.   Names of applicants for a bail bondsman license will be forwarded to sheriffs, police chiefs and prosecutors for references. Negative replies shall be investigated to determine if licensing infractions exist.

E.   Company licensees will go through the same procedure as a bail bondsman licensee in regard to letters to sheriffs, police chiefs and prosecutors. This applies to all sole proprietors, partners, stockholders and officers.

F.   Any application for a company license will be approved or denied by the Board.

G.   There will be no fictitious names used in the bail bond business. Company applications containing fictitious names will be returned.

H.   Applicants for a bail bondsman license will be approved or denied by the Board or its designee.

I.   In the case of a bail bondsman's application being denied by the Board Designee, the applicant can appeal the decision to the Board.

J.   Applicants for an initial bail bondsman license who satisfactorily complete the examination and meet the other qualifications and requirements prescribed by law, including eight (8) hours of beginning education, shall be licensed by the Board.

SECTION 16.   LICENSE REQUIRED

A.   A licensed bail bondsman must carry a current copy of his/her company's license, his/her bail bondsman license and a current copy of his/her Qualifying Power of Attorney and must present same, when initiating a bail bond if documents are requested by authorized person(s).

B.   The signature of the bail bondsman issuing the bond must be affixed to the bond. Bonds shall not be pre-signed by the bail bondsman nor shall any licensee sign another bail bondsman's name.

C.   Any licensed bail bondsman or licensed bail bond company who permits any person not so licensed to solicit or engage in the bail bond business in his/her/its behalf or any professional bail bond company or professional bail bondsman who permits any bail bond to be executed to effect the release of a defendant without being physically present shall be deemed in violation of Ark. Code Ann. Section 17-19-201.

D.   The definition of bail bond business shall not include individuals employed solely for the performance of clerical, stenographic, investigative or other administrative duties if the employee's compensation is not related to the number of bail bonds written. Notwithstanding the foregoing, no person whose bail bondsman license has been revoked may be employed by a bail bond company in any capacity. Additionally, no member, officer or director of a bail bond company whose license has been revoked may be employed by a bail bond company in any capacity, unless the Board entered a specific finding of fact in the matter that the member, officer or director was not personally at fault and did not acquiesce in the matter on account of which the company license was revoked as provided by Ark. Code Ann. § 17-19-210(g).

SECTION 17. TRANSFER OF BAIL BONDSMAN LICENSE

A bail bondsman who desires to transfer his license from one company to another shall:

A. Pay a transfer fee of two hundred fifty dollars ($250) to the board; and

B. File with the board:

(i)   A sworn affidavit stating that all premiums, fees, and powers of attorney owed to or issued by the company from which the bail bondsman is transferring his or her license have been delivered to the company;

(ii)   A letter of resignation addressed to the company from which the bail bondsman is transferring or a letter of termination addressed to the bail bondsman from the company terminating the bail bondsman's appointment;

(iii)   A completed bail bondsman application on forms prescribed by the board;

(iv)   A completed company statement from the company to which the bail bondsman desires to transfer his or her license; and

(v)   An original qualifying power of attorney issued by the company to which the bail bondsman desires to transfer his or her license.

C.   Upon receipt of a request for transfer of a bail bondsman license, the transfer fee and the documents specified in (B) above, the board shall forward copies of the letter of resignation, if applicable, and the sworn affidavit of the bail bondsman to the company from which the bail bondsman desires to transfer his or her license.

D.   Upon receipt of the documents specified in (C) above, the company from which the bail bondsman is transferring shall have seven (7) business days in which to contest the bail bondsman's sworn statement.

E.   A company contesting a bail bondsman's sworn statement shall file a written complaint on forms furnished by the board setting out in detail the property the company denies the bail bondsman has returned.

F.   Any documents supporting the complaint that shall be offered as evidence to prove the complaint shall be attached to the complaint.

G.   Upon receipt of the complaint, the executive director shall set the matter for an informal hearing to be held within seven (7) days of receipt of the complaint and notify the company filing the complaint and the bail bondsman by certified mail, return receipt requested, of the date, time and location of the informal hearing.

H.   Either party may appeal the decision of the executive director to a formal hearing before the board by filing a written notice of appeal with the board within seven (7) days of receipt of the executive director's decision.

I.   No transfer of a bail bondsman's license shall be effective prior to the expiration of the seven (7) day period for contesting the transfer request unless the company from which the bail bondman is requesting a transfer shall notify the board it has no objection to the transfer, in which case the transfer may be entered prior to the expiration of the seven (7) day period.

  (i) If no complaint contesting the bail bondsman's transfer is received during the seven (7) day contest period, the license shall be transferred as requested.

  (ii) A company that does not contest the sworn affidavit of a transferring bail bondsman is not precluded by the failure to contest the sworn affidavit from filing a complaint that alleges a violation of the applicable statutes, rules, by the transferring bail bondsman upon discovery of the alleged violation by the company.

J.   If the allegations of a complaint contesting the transfer are found to have been established, no transfer of the license shall be accomplished until the bail bondsman accounts for, returns, or pays to the professional bail bond company contesting the transfer the property or money issued to or held in a fiduciary capacity by the bail bondsman.

  (i) If a complaint contesting the transfer is filed, a specific finding of fact shall be made concerning whether the affidavit or complaint contesting the affidavit was filed in good faith by the respective parties.

  (ii) In the case of a finding of a lack of good faith, the party to whom the finding applies shall be subject to sanctions or disciplinary action pursuant to the provisions of Ark. Code Ann. Section 17-19-210 and as provided by applicable rules.

SECTION 18. LICENSE RENEWAL, CONTINUING EDUCATION REQUIRED

A. All Professional Bail Bond Company licenses issued pursuant to Ark. Code Ann. § 17-19-101 et. seq. expire on December 31 of every year. Renewal of professional bail bond company and professional bail bondsman licenses is required prior to December 31 to prevent expiration.

B. Every Arkansas licensed bail bond company shall submit its renewal packet by December 1 of each year to ensure renewal of both the company license and the bail bondsman licenses by January 1 of the next year.

C. Renewal packets received after December 1 will be processed; however, a penalty of one hundred dollars ($100.00) per day will be assessed until the packet is received, beginning December 2 and continuing through December 31.

D. Company and bondsman renewal applications received after December 15 but prior to December 31 will be processed on the corresponding day in January of the following year. (Example: Packet received December 16 will be processed on January 16 of next year). No bonds shall be issued by any company or bondsman after December 31 until the new license is issued and received by the bond company/bondsman.

E. Renewal applications for a Professional Bail Bond Company or for a Professional Bail Bondsman license received after December 31 will be treated as applications for initial license. All applicants will be treated as applicants for a new license and will have to complete the entire licensing process.

F. Licensees shall annually complete not fewer than six (6) hours of continuing education courses presented by a Board approved provider.

G. Bondsmen who fail to complete the required continuing education program will not be re-licensed for the upcoming year. Those bondsmen desiring to have their licenses reinstated must attend a continuing education class offered in the current licensing year before a license will be issued. A second continuing education class must be attended in order for the bondsman to obtain a license for the following year.

SECTION 19.   LICENSE DENIAL – COMPANY

A.   A bail bond company license shall not be issued or renewed, and may be revoked, if any owner, partner, stockholder or officer:

1.   Has been convicted of a felony or any offense involving moral turpitude;

2.   Is regularly or frequently employed by:

(a) A court of law; or

(b) A public law enforcement agency;

3.   Is an attorney licensed by the State of Arkansas or an employee of an attorney;

4.   Is a person or entity found by the Board to be incompetent, untrustworthy, financially irresponsible or of doubtful personal and business reputation;

5.   Is a person or entity whose license has been previously revoked.

B.   A company owner having knowledge that another licensee has committed a violation of these rules or any statute regulating bail bonds, bail bondsman or bail bond companies, or has been convicted of a felony or other offense which would disqualify the licensee from holding such license shall promptly notify the Board.

SECTION 20.   LICENSE DENIAL – BONDSMAN

A.   A bail bondsman's license shall not be issued or renewed to any individual, and may be revoked, if that individual:

1. Has been convicted of a felony or any offense involving moral turpitude.

2. Is regularly or frequently employed by:

(a) A court of law; or

(b) A public law enforcement agency.

3. Is an attorney licensed by the State of Arkansas or an employee of an attorney.

4. Is found by the Board to be incompetent, untrustworthy, financially irresponsible or of doubtful personal and business reputation;

5. Is a person whose license has been previously revoked.

SECTION 21. FINANCIAL STATEMENTS; GUIDELINES

A.   Assets listed on the financial statement of a corporation seeking to be licensed or re-licensed shall be assets directly owned by the corporation and held in the name of such corporation.

B.   Assets listed on the financial statement of a partnership seeking licensure or re-licensure as a professional bail bond company shall be those assets owned by the partnership; assets owned individually by one partner may be listed as long as such assets are identified separately on the financial statement.

C.   Assets listed on the financial statement of a sole proprietorship shall be those personally owned and held by such sole proprietor.

D.   Certificates of Deposit filed with the Board pursuant to Ark. Code Ann. Section 17-19-205(a)(1) must be identified on financial statements. When the certificate of deposit is not an asset of the company, the ownership of the certificate and any agreement between the company and the owner of the certificate of deposit must be disclosed to the Board.

E.   Assets of the Company that secure a Clean Irrevocable Letter of Credit filed with the Board pursuant to Ark. Code Ann. Section 17-19-205(a)(1) must be identified on financial statements. When the company does not own the assets securing a Clean Irrevocable Letter of Credit, the ownership of such assets and any agreement between the company and the owner of such assets must be disclosed to the Board.

F.   Any real or personal property listed as an asset must be property not subject to the exemption laws of this state, unless a waiver to said exemption has been properly executed and filed with the financial statement.

G.   Notes receivable from arrestees and principals shall not be considered an asset.

H.   Property held as collateral on a bond shall not be considered an asset.

I.   The Board may request any documentation to verify the worth of any asset listed or to show the extent of any encumbrance or the lack of any encumbrance.

J.   Any real or personal property valued at more than $10,000.00 shall be shown at its current appraised valuation unless such asset is in the form of cash or bank deposits; then the value shall be the property's actual value, or in the case of bonds or publicly traded stock, the actual market value.

K.   Licensees listing stocks issued by closely held corporations and/or which are not publicly traded must include a written statement of the stock valuation from a corporate officer and a current audited financial statement. Any appraisal or financial statement submitted shall be from a qualified, independent and objective source.

SECTION 22.   COLLATERAL; FIDUCIARY RELATIONSHIP

A.   When a bail bond company/agent takes physical possession of collateral, a pre-numbered written receipt must be given reflecting the following:

(1) the name, address and telephone number of the professional bail bond company;

(2) the name and signature of the person giving collateral;

(3) the bail bond number(s) for which collateral is posted;

(4) a description and approximate value of collateral received;

(5) the purpose for collateral received; and

(6) the name and signature of the bail bond agent.

B.   Any licensee who receives collateral in connection with a bail transaction shall receive such collateral in a fiduciary capacity, and, prior to any forfeiture of bail, shall keep it separate and apart from any other funds or assets of such licensee.

C.   At no time shall collateral be converted to the personal use of the licensee or bail bond company prior to any forfeiture.

SECTION 23. RETURN OF EXCESS COLLATERAL ON FORFEITURE; EXPENSES

A. If collateral received is in excess of the bail forfeited, such excess shall be returned to the person who placed the collateral with the licensee immediately upon the application of the collateral to the forfeiture.

B. Documented reasonable expenses incurred due to a breach of the bail bond contract or Court Order may be deducted from the collateral, if the Court does not allow a remission from the sum specified in the bail bond.

SECTION 24. REFUND OF PREMIUM

The principal shall be entitled to a refund of his premium when the arrestee is surrendered by his bail bondsman at any time prior to the final termination of the liability of the bond provided that the arrestee has not committed any of the following:

 A. Left the jurisdiction of the court without written consent of the court for a period in excess of twenty-four (24) hours;

 B. Moved from his place of residence without notifying his bail bondsman;

 C. Was arrested for an offense other than a traffic violation;

 D. Violated any substantive provision in the bail bond contract.

The principal shall be entitled to a refund of his premium when the bail bondsman fails to secure the defendant's release from actual custody.

SECTION 25. ALLOWABLE CHARGES

A. The premium allowed by Ark. Code Ann. Section 17-19-301 is the maximum amount a bail bondsman may charge for writing a bond.

B. The following separate charges are not allowable and shall not be charged by a company or any licensee:

(1) Operating expenses
(2) Mileage
(3) Telephone calls
(4) Photo fees
(5) Postage
(6) Extra personnel fees
(7) Prepaid recovery expenses

C.   Allowable charges do include any expenses such as filing fees for documents or other fees that are expenses incurred by the person executing any documents in order to procure coverage by a bail bond.

D.   Any rebating or discounting of premiums by any company or licensee is strictly prohibited.

SECTION 26.   FORFEITURES; MISREPRESENTATIONS

No bail bondsman shall purposely make any misleading or untrue representations to any court or to any public official for the purpose of avoiding or preventing a forfeiture of bail or setting aside a forfeiture that has already occurred.

SECTION 27.   UNPAID FORFEITURES AND MISCONDUCT; LICENSE SANCTIONS

A.   If it is found that any licensee has been found guilty of misconduct or malfeasance and upon notice from the aggrieved party of damages due to the licensee's misconduct, the Board may notify the licensee by certified mail of the claim.

(1) If the verified amount due the aggrieved party is not paid within twenty (20) days of issuance of notice, the Board may suspend the license and immediately withdraw the allowable amount from the posted certificate of deposit or maintain a civil action on the letter of credit.

(2) The license of the malefactor shall remain suspended until the amount of damage is paid.

(3) If the amount remains unpaid after suspension, the Board may order a hearing for the licensee to show cause why his license should not be revoked.

(4) Any company whose license is revoked by the Board pursuant to a show cause hearing must immediately discontinue operations. Telephone service, signs and other forms of advertising and communication shall be disconnected and the offices locked.

B.   When a final civil judgment of forfeiture is entered as to a bail bond issued by a licensee by a court of competent jurisdiction and the judgment is not paid within ninety (90) days thereafter and is forwarded to the Board pursuant to Ark. Code Ann. Section 17-19-208(b)(1), the Board shall notify the licensee involved by certified mail. If the forfeiture judgment remains unpaid for ten (10) days following issuance of notice, the Board may administratively suspend the license and make claim against the licensee's security deposit up to the allowable amount of ten thousand dollars ($10,000.00).

SECTION 28.   BAIL BOND COMPLAINT FORM AND PROCEDURES

A.   Complaints may be filed and hearings will be conducted pursuant to A.C.A. § 17-19-209 and Act 1477 of 1999.

B.   Any person desiring to make a complaint concerning an alleged violation of Ark. Code Ann. Sections 17-19-201, et seq., by any company or bondsman shall use the bail bond complaint form prescribed in Appendix "G" of this rule. A copy of the complaint form may be obtained from the Board.

C.   The form must be signed by the complaining party under penalty of perjury and be notarized.

SECTION 29.   COMPLAINTS, COOPERATION REQUIRED

A.   All complaints will be investigated by the Executive Director or his/her designee.

B.   Every bail bondsman and company shall promptly respond to all correspondence, request for information, or otherwise, directed to the bondsman or company by the Board or an employee thereof. Every licensed professional bail bondsman and/or company shall fully cooperate with any examination or investigation conducted by the Board.

C.   Failure on the part of any company or its licensees to make all financial and business records available for inspection or examination upon request by the Board, or failure to otherwise cooperate, may be grounds for a hearing.

D.   If any person or company regulated by this Board files a complaint or causes a complaint to be filed against another person or company regulated by this Board and said complaint is ultimately determined by the Board to be a complaint without merit, the complaining party shall be brought before this Board for appropriate disciplinary action pursuant to Ark. Code Ann. Section17-19-210.

SECTION 30.   HEARING OFFICER

The Board may appoint a hearing officer to preside at hearings pursuant to A.C.A. §25-15-213 and who may, if authorized by the Board, prepare a proposal for decision pursuant to A.C.A. §25-15-210.

SECTION 31.   HEARINGS, REVOCATION OR SUSPENSION OF LICENSE

A.   All hearings shall be conducted in the same manner as hearings held by the Board under the Arkansas Administrative Procedure Act, Ark. Code Ann. Section 25-15-201 et seq., unless otherwise stated.

B.   At the discretion of the Board, the Executive Director may hold informal hearings in reference to a complaint or the Executive Director may set a formal hearing before the Board. The company or bondsman may request a formal hearing before the Board. Consent agreements entered into as a result of an informal hearing shall be submitted for Board approval at the next regularly scheduled meeting of the Board after the informal hearing.

C.   The Board may subpoena witnesses; administer oaths and affirmations; examine any individual under oath; require and compel production of books, papers, contracts and other documents. Subpoenas of witnesses shall be served in the same manner as if issued by a circuit court and may be served by certified mail.

D.   If any individual fails to obey a subpoena, duly issued and served, with respect to any matter concerning which he or she may be lawfully interrogated, the Board may apply to the Pulaski County Circuit Court which may issue an order requiring the individual to comply with the subpoena and to testify. Failure to obey the order of the court may be punished by the court as a contempt thereof.

E.	Any person willfully testifying falsely under oath to any matter material to any examination, investigation, or hearing shall, upon conviction, be guilty of perjury and punished accordingly.

F.	Notice of the time and place of the hearing, stating the matters to be considered shall be given not less than ten (10) days in advance.

G.	The Board shall allow any party to the hearing to appear in person and by counsel, to be present during the giving of all evidence, to have a reasonable opportunity to inspect all documentary evidence and to examine witnesses, to present evidence in support of his or her interest, and to have subpoenas issued by the Board to compel attendance of witnesses and production of evidence in his or her behalf.

H.	The Board may suspend for up to twelve (12) months or revoke or refuse to continue any license, if after notice and hearing the Board determines that the licensee or any member of a company has violated any provision of Ark. Code Ann. Section 17-19-210.

I.	The acts or conduct of any bondsman who acts within the scope of the authority delegated to him or her shall be deemed the act or conduct of the company for which the bondsman is acting as agent.

J.	If the Board finds that one (1) or more grounds exist for the suspension or revocation of any license, the board may request that formal charges be filed against the violator and that the penalties set out in Ark. Code Ann. Section 17-19-102 be imposed.

K.	If the If the Board finds that one (1) or more grounds exist for the suspension or revocation of any license and that the license has been suspended within the previous twenty-four (24) months, the license shall be revoked.

L.	The Board may not again issue a license to any person or entity whose license has been revoked.

M.	If the Board or its designee determines that the public health, safety or welfare imperatively requires emergency action, and incorporates a finding to that effect in its order, a summary suspension of a licensee may be ordered pending an administrative hearing before the Board, which shall be promptly instituted.

N.	If a company license is suspended or revoked, no member of the company or officer or director of the corporation shall be licensed or be designated in any license to exercise the powers thereof during the period of suspension or revocation, unless the Board determines upon substantial evidence that the member, officer, or director was not personally at fault and did not acquiesce in the matter on account of which the license was suspended or revoked.

O.   A party may appeal from any order of the Board as a matter of right. The appeal shall be taken to the Pulaski County Circuit Court by filing written notice of appeal to the Court and by filing a copy of the notice with the Board within thirty (30) days after issuance of the Order by the Board.

P.   Within thirty (30) days after filing of the copy of the notice of appeal with the Board, the Board shall make, certify and deposit in the office of the clerk of the court in which the appeal is pending a full and complete transcript of all proceedings had before the Board and all evidence before the Board in the matter, including all of the Board's files therein.

SECTION 32.   GIFTS PROHIBITED

A.   No licensee shall give, directly or indirectly, any gift of any kind to any public official, any candidate for public office, or any employee of a governmental agency who has duties or responsibilities with respect to the administration of justice or a place where in detention of a person charged with a crime may occur or to any prisoner in any jail.

B.   Items that are distributed generally for the purposes of advertising and political contributions lawfully given shall not be considered gifts for the purposes of this section.

SECTION 33.   NOTICE OF CHANGE OF ADDRESS

A.   Every professional bail bondsman and professional bail bond company shall notify the Board in writing of any change of his/her/its principal business address and/or his/her residence address within thirty (30) days of such change.

B.   Failure to notify the Board of such address change may be grounds for a hearing.

SECTION 34.   WRITTEN STATEMENT OF BAIL TRANSACTION; CONTENTS

Every bail bondsman shall, at the time of obtaining the release of an arrestee on bail, deliver (and keep a copy for his own records) to such arrestee or to the principal a numbered document signed by the arrestee containing the following information as prescribed in Appendix "C":

(1)   the name of the bail bondsman;

(2)   the name, address and telephone number of the professional bail bond company;

(3)   the name of the arrestee;

(4)   the date of arrest;

(5)   the date of release of the arrestee;

(6)   the date, time and place of the arrestee's required appearance, if known;

(7)   the amount of bail;

(8)   the offenses with which the arrestee is charged;

(9)   the premium for the bail bond;

(10)   the amount received;

(11)   the unpaid balance, if any; and

(12)   a description of and receipt number for any collateral received.

SECTION 35.   EXAMINATIONS

After a person passes the examination for licensure, he shall have one (1) year from the date the examination result is certified to apply for a license. If he applies for a license more than one (1) year from the date the examination result is certified, he shall be required to retake and pass the examination before a license can be issued.

SECTION 36.   RECORD RETENTION

All records required herein shall be maintained for a period of five (5) years at one central location. If the records are kept at a location other than the mailing address on file at the Board, such address must be submitted to the Board in writing with a notation that such address is where the records are maintained.

SECTION 37.   COMPANY APPOINTMENT

A.   A professional bail bondsman can represent no more than one professional bail bond company at a time.

B.   A company that notifies the Board it has terminated the appointment of a bail bondsman must wait a minimum of seven (7) days after notice of termination before requesting reinstatement of the bondsman's license.

SECTION 38.   ADVERTISING

A.   All advertising pursuant to Ark. Code Ann. Section 17-19-109 shall prominently display the company name, i.e., the company name shall be larger than the agent's name. (See Appendix "H".)

B.   There will be no fictitious names used in the bail bond business. All advertising will be in the name of the licensed company only.

C.   Companies shall annually provide the Board a list containing the physical address and phone number of its offices or business locations publicly displaying advertising. The list shall be included in the company's renewal application.

D.   When a bail bond office or business location publicly displaying advertising changes addresses or closes or a new bail bond office or business location publicly displaying advertising is opened, the company must notify the Board within thirty days of such address change, closing, or opening of the new bail bond office or business location.

SECTION 39.   APPREHENSION OF DEFENDANTS

A.   No person shall represent himself/herself to be a bail enforcement agent, bounty hunter or similar title.

B.   No professional bail bond company/bondsman shall permit or authorize any person to apprehend a defendant on bail unless that person is qualified pursuant to A.C.A. §16-84-114 and is:

1.   A bail bond agent licensed by the state where the bond was written; or

2.   A private investigator licensed in Arkansas; or

3.   A certified law enforcement officer; or

4. A person who is acting under the direct supervision of an Arkansas licensed bail bondsman and who is at least twenty-one (21) years of age with no prior felony convictions or convictions for any offense involving moral turpitude or violence.

C. Any bail bond company/bail bondsman permitting or authorizing a person other than the surety to apprehend or surrender a defendant pursuant to A.C.A. §16-84-114(3)(b) must provide the agent with:

1. Written authorization on company letterhead using the form approved by the Board and contained in Appendix "É" of this rule; and

2. A certified copy of the bail bond or recognizance appropriately endorsed as provided in A.C.A. §16-84-114.

D. Any bail bondsman or agent authorized pursuant to Ark. Code Ann. Section 16-84-114 attempting to apprehend a defendant must notify the local law enforcement agency or agencies of his presence and provide them with the defendant's name, charges and suspected location

E. The bondsman or agent shall record the date and time of notification and the identity of the law enforcement agency official to whom notification was given.

F. Notification must be given prior to any apprehension attempt, to a law enforcement official on duty, at least once every forty-eight (48) hours during the apprehension attempt or as required by policies of the law enforcement agency to which notice is given.

SECTION 40.   COMPLIANCE WITH POSTED RULES OF JAILS

A. A licensee shall comply with publicly posted rules of a jail.

B. As used in this section, "Rules" shall mean policies and procedures relating to the operation of a jail that are not in conflict with state or federal statutes and that have been approved by the chief law enforcement officer of the jail.

C. A licensee who is found, after notice and hearing, to have violated this sections may be subject to disciplinary action as provided in Ark. Code Ann. § 17-19-210 (2001 Repl.).

SECTION 41. SEVERABILITY

Any section or provision of this rule held by the court to be invalid or unconstitutional will not affect the validity of any other section or provision.

APPENDICES TO RULE AND REGULATION 1

Appendix A – Bail Bond Form. 93

Appendix B – Affidavit of Sole Proprietorship. 94

Appendix C – Statement of Bail and Payment Received.. 95

Appendix D – Qualifying Power of Attorney. 96

Appendix E – Quarterly Report Form. 97

Appendix F – Clean Irrevocable Letter of Credit. 99

Appendix G – Bail Bond Complaint Form. 102

Appendix H – Advertising Examples. 104

Appendix I – Authorization by Surety to Arrest Defendant on Bail Bond. 105

Appendix J – Collateral Receipt (Example). 106

APPENDIX A

STATE OF ARKANSAS   NAME OF COMPANY   **BAIL BOND**
COUNTY OF_____   ADDRESS OF COMPANY
CITY OF_____   CITY, STATE, ZIP CODE   XX_____-_____
CASE NUMBER_____   (AREA CODE) PHONE NUMBER

_____,hereinafter referred to as the Defendant, being in custody, charged with the
_____Item 5 – defendant
offense(s) of_____

and having been admitted to bail in the amount of $_____.

Now ___NAME OF COMPANY_____does hereby undertake that the Defendant will appear before the Court designated below at the time indicated and shall at all times
render himself amenable to the orders and process of said court in prosecution of charges, and if convicted, shall render himself in execution thereof. If the Defendant
fails to perform any of these conditions, we will pay and forfeit to the _____court of _____, the sum of
$_____
                                                    (County or District to be Inserted)

In Witness Whereof I have hereunto set my hand and seal this_____day of_____, 20_____.
_____   Defendant:_____

Defendant to Appear In: Address:_____

District Court, City of_____   City, State, Zip:_____

District Court, County of_____   Phone:_____

At_____A.M./P.M. on_____, 20_____   Surety: ___NAME OF COMPANY_____
_____County Circuit Court   _____
                                                                Attorney-In-Fact   (agent)
On NOTICE TERM_____

Power of Attorney

Authority for:	Item 1	Item 2	Item 3	Item 4	Power Number
		Not valid for Bond in excess of $	Not valid If used after	Date Issued	XX_____00001
_____ To act as Attorney-In-Fact – State of Arkansas					

DEFENDANT:		Insert Bond Amount Void if Not Completed
SOCIAL SECURITY #:	DATE OF BIRTH	$

Know All Men By These Presents:

SECTION 1.____NAME OF COMPANY_____, (a Sole Proprietorship/Partnership/Incorporation), does hereby make, constitute and appoint the party set forth in Item One (1) above as its true and lawful Attorney-in-Fact with full power and authority hereby confirmed to execute on behalf of the said Company, as sole surety only subject to the limitations as herein set forth, Bail Bonds, in judicial proceedings, whether criminal or civil; appeal bonds or any other kind of appearance bond in any State Court, or District Court and in all U.S. Federal Courts on behalf of the above named defendant.
SECTION 2. That the authority of such Attorney-in-Fact to bind the company shall not in any event exceed the amount set forth in Item Two (2) above on any one bond and the said Attorney-in-Fact is hereby authorized to insert in Item Five (5) the name of the person on whose behalf this bond is given.
SECTION 3. This power is not valid unless used on or before the date set forth in Item Three (3) above and can only be used once.
SECTION 4. The authority of such Attorney-in-Fact is limited to appearance bonds and cannot be construed to guarantee failure to provide payments, back alimony payments, child support payments, fines or wage law claims.
SECTION 5.____NAME OF COMPANY_____, does make, constitute and appoint the above named agent its true and lawful Attorney-in-Fact for it and in its name, place and stead, to execute, seal and deliver for and on its behalf and as its act and deed, as surety, a bail bond only. Authority of such Attorney-in-Fact is limited to appearance bonds and cannot be construed to guarantee failure to provide payments, fines or wage law claims on behalf of above named defendant.
SECTION 6. IN WITNESS WHEREOF_____NAME OF COMPANY_____has caused these presents to be signed by its Proprietor and its corporate seal to be hereunto affixed (if applicable) on the date set forth in Item Four (4) above.
SECTION 7. DO NOT ACCEPT A POWER OF ATTORNEY WHICH BEARS ANY ALTERATIONS, ERASURE OR INTERLINEATION.
(A) Bail Bond Form with Incorporated Power of Attorney should remain a permanent part of Court Records.

_____ OWNER

APPENDIX B

STATE OF ARKANSAS
COUNTY OF_____
CITY OF_____
CASE NUMBER_____

NAME OF COMPANY
ADDRESS OF COMPANY
CITY, STATE, ZIP CODE
(AREA CODE) PHONE NUMBER

BAIL BOND

XX___-_____

_____,hereinafter referred to as the Defendant, being in custody, charged with the
        Item 5 – defendant

offense(s) of_____

and having been admitted to bail in the amount of $_____.

Now __NAME OF COMPANY_____does hereby undertake that the Defendant will appear before the Court designated below at the time indicated and shall at all times
render himself amenable to the orders and process of said court in prosecution of charges, and if convicted, shall render himself in execution thereof. If the Defendant
fails to perform any of these conditions, we will pay and forfeit to the _____court of _____, the sum of
$_____
                                                                                (County or District to be Inserted)

        In Witness Whereof I have hereunto set my hand and seal this_____day of_____, 20_____.
_____   Defendant:_____

Defendant to Appear In: Address:_____

District Court, City of_____   City, State, Zip:_____

District Court, County of_____   Phone:_____

At_____A.M./P.M. on_____, 20_____   Surety: ___NAME OF COMPANY_____

_____County Circuit Court   _____
                                                                        Attorney-In-Fact   (agent)
On NOTICE TERM_____

Affidavit of Sole Proprietorship

Authority for: Item 1	Item 2	Item 3	Item 4	Power Number
	Not valid for Bond in excess of $	Not valid If used after	Date Issued	XX_____00001
_____ To act as Attorney-In-Fact – State of Arkansas				

			Insert Bond Amount Void if Not Completed
DEFENDANT:			
SOCIAL SECURITY #:	DATE OF BIRTH		$

AFFIDAVIT OF SOLE PROPRIETORSHIP:

STATE OF ARKANSAS
COUNTY OF_____

_____NAME OF SOLE PROPRIETOR_____ being duly sworn upon oath, deposes and affirms as follows: That I am a resident of the State of

Arkansas. That I am the proprietor of _____NAME OF COMPANY_____, a Professional Bail Bond Company, and that such Company will operate

in this State solely as a proprietorship, and that I am responsible for the acts, liabilities, and operations of said company.

                                        _____
                                                        Name

                                        _____
                                                        Date

Subscribed and sworn to or affirmed before me this _____day of _____, 20_____.

_____
My Commission Expires   Notary Public

APPENDIX C

. . . .

Statement of Bail and Payment Received

NAME OF COMPANY, ADDRESS, CITY, STATE, ZIP CODE   (AREA CODE) PHONE NUMBER   XX___001

Date: _____ Agent: _____ Bond # _____

Arrestee: _____ DOB: _____

        Last   First   Middle

Date & Time of Arrest: _____ A.M./P.M.   Date & Time of Release _____A.M./P.M.

Court: _____   Appearance Date & Time: _____ A.M./P.M.

Charges _____   Amount of Bail _____

_____   Premium _____

       Collateral: NO □   YES □   Collateral Receipt # _____   Filing Fee _____

Arrestee: _____   State Fee _____

Agent: _____   TOTAL _____

Co-Signer _____   Amount Paid _____

Co-Signer _____   Balance Due _____

APPENDIX D

_____

_____

No._____

QUALIFYING POWER OF ATTORNEY

KNOW ALL MEN BY THESE PRESENTS: That (Name of Company) a (Corporation) (or Partnership) (or Sole Proprietorship) having its principal office at _____(City)_____, _____(State)_____ does hereby make, constitute and appoint_____(Agent)_____, with limited authority, its true and lawful Agent and Attorney-in-Fact, with full power and authority hereby conferred to sign, execute, acknowledge, and deliver for and on its behalf as Surety, subject to the limitations herein set forth, any and all papers and documents necessary or incidental to making of Bail Bonds in Judicial Proceedings, whether criminal or civil; appeal bonds or any other kind of appearance bond in any State Court, County Court or District Court, not to exceed the amount of

$(Insert Power Amount)

for any and all bail bonds and recognizances, provided that the said Attorney-in-Fact shall attach to every bond or undertaking a separate numbered Power of Attorney designating his authority; otherwise, said bond or undertaking shall be deemed null and void. A specimen copy of said separate numbered Power of Attorney is attached hereto.

The acknowledgment and execution of any such documentation by the said Attorney-in-Fact shall be binding upon this Company.

IN WITNESS WHEREOF, The said (Name of Company) has caused these presents to be executed by (Name and Title of Corporate Officer/ Partner/ Proprietor)   this _____ day of _____, 20_____.

_____
(Name of Company)

_____
(Corporate Officer, Partner or Proprietor)

State of Arkansas   )
)ss
County of _____)

On this _____ day of _____, 20_____, before me, a Notary Public, personally appeared _____, who being by me duly sworn, acknowledged that he/she signed the above Powers of Attorney as Authorized Representative of the said (Name of Company)_____ and acknowledged said instruments to be the voluntary act and deed of said Company.

My Commission Expires:

_____   _____
                                                Notary Public

                                 _____
                                                Agent/Attorney-in-Fact

APPENDIX E

QUARTERLY REPORT FORM
BONDS DISCHARGED/EXONERATED

COMPANY NAME:_____COMPANY#_____FROM_____TO_____, 20__

AGENT#	DEFENDANT'S NAME	BOND#	DATE WRITTEN	COURT	AMT. OF BOND	AMOUNT SEC/ UNSEC.	DATE EXONERATED

*Continue columns to make full pages.

QUARTERLY REPORT FORM
BONDS WRITTEN

COMPANY NAME:_____COMPANY#_____FROM_____TO_____, 20__.

AGENT #	DEFENDANT NAME	CHARGES AGAINST DEFENDANT	BOND #	DATE WRITTEN	TO WHOM WRITTEN	COURT	AMT. OF BOND	AMT. UNSECURED	AMT. SECURED	HOW SECURED

*Continue columns to make full page

APPENDIX E
(Page 2)

QUARTERLY REPORT FORM
LIABILITY SUMMARY

COMPANY NAME:_____

COMPANY #_____FROM_____TO_____, 20____

      Outstanding Unsecured Liability Last Report $_____

Unsecured   Bonds Written This Report $_____ _____

      Unsecured Bonds Discharged/Exonerated This Report $_____

      Total Outstanding Unsecured Liability $_____

      Outstanding Secured Liability Last Report $_____

Secured   Bonds Written This Report $_____ _____

      Secured Bonds Discharged/Exonerated This Report $_____

      Total Outstanding Secured Liability $_____

   Total Outstanding liability $_____

Number   of Bonds Used This Report   _____   _____

     Number of Bonds Voided This Report   _____

Number   of Bonds Written This Report   _____   _____

APPENDIX F

CLEAN IRREVOCABLE LETTER OF CREDIT

_____
_____
_____
_____
(Name and address of issuer if not on letterhead)

_____
Date

Arkansas Professional Bail Bondsman Licensing Board
101 East Capitol, Suite 117
Little Rock, Arkansas 72201

Re: Clean Irrevocable Letter of Credit No._____

     Expiration Date_____

Dear Board:

At the request of_____, a professional bail bond company ("Company"), we, as issuer, are opening a Clean Irrevocable Letter of Credit in favor of you or your successors in office for up to the aggregate amount of _____ ($_____), or such amount as indicated by the Addendum attached hereto, or any amendments thereof. We undertake that drawings under this Letter of Credit for any liability incurred by Company during term of this Letter of Credit shall be honored upon presentation of a draft to issuer *by you or your authorized representative. Drawings shall be honored by Issuer whether presented prior to the expiration date of the Letter of Credit or after the term of the Letter of Credit has expired. Issuer agrees and acknowledges that its obligation under this Letter of Credit matures at the time Company or any of its licensees fail to faithfully perform their duties as required by law. All drafts so drawn must be marked drawn under the above referenced Credit Number.

This Letter of Credit, which is retroactive from _____, is issued to you or your successors in office to meet the requirements of Ark. Code Ann. §17-19-205, which requires each bail bond company license applicant and renewal company license applicant to post and maintain with the Arkansas Professional Bail Bondsman Licensing Board a security deposit.

If during the term of this Letter of Credit, any of the licensees listed in the Addendum attached hereto are guilty of failing to faithfully perform their duties as required by law, the Board may draw upon this Letter of Credit pursuant to Ark. Code Ann. §17-19-208 and either recover the full amount of the penalty incurred or bond forfeited, or recover for the use and benefit of the person or persons aggrieved, the amount of loss or injury sustained by such person or persons by reason of such misconduct or forfeited bond. However, no such recovery or recoveries shall exceed a maximum amount of Ten Thousand Dollars ($10,000.00) as stated in Ark. Code Ann. §17-19-208.

It is a condition of this Letter of Credit that it shall not be subject to termination, expiration or cancellation in less than sixty (60) days after giving written notice thereof by certified mail, return receipt requested, to the Arkansas Professional Bail Bondsman Licensing Board.

It is a condition of this Letter of Credit that it shall be deemed automatically extended without amendment from any expiration date stated herein, unless sixty (60) days prior to any such date we shall notify you or your successors in office in writing by certified mail, return receipt requested, that we elect not to consider this Letter of Credit renewed for any such additional period.

It is a condition of this Letter of Credit that no such termination or cancellation or non-renewal shall affect the liability of the Issuer incurred prior to the effective date of such termination or cancellation or non-renewal. Issuer's liability under this Letter of Credit is incurred at the time Company or any of its licensees fail to faithfully perform their duties as required by law.

It is a further condition of the Letter of Credit that it is issued to the Board solely for the express obligations of licensees as enumerated under Ark. Code Ann. §17-19-205, therefore it is expressly agreed and acknowledged by the Issuer that only the Board's drafts drawn under and in compliance with the terms of this Letter will be duly honored by the Issuer if presented as set forth herein. The Issuer confirms the credit and hereby undertakes that all such drafts drawn and presented will be duly honored.

It is understood and acknowledged by the Issuer herein that the list of bail bond licensees who are the subject of this Letter of Credit and who are named in the attached Addendum, may change from time to time due to normal personnel changes. Therefore, it is agreed by the Issuer that such additions and deletions of licensed personnel shall be reflected by amending the attached Addendum and by affixing the revision date and wet signature of an officer of the Issuer.

Except as expressly stated otherwise, this credit is subject to the "Uniform Customs and Practice for Documentary Credit", 1993 Revision of the International Chamber of Commerce, Publication No. 500.

Sincerely,

_____
Officer of the Issuer

_____
Title or Position

ADDENDUM

Name of Bail Bond Company _____

Issuer _____   Date/Amount of Original Letter of Credit
       _____
       _____

                                        Credit No._____

Covered Licensee(s):

Officer of the Issuer   _____

                                        _____
                                                Title or Position

                                        _____

                                                Date

ARKANSAS PROFESSIONAL BAIL BOND LICENSING BOARD

COMPLAINT FORM

COMPLAINING PARTY

1. Name_____

Address_____

       City_____State_____

       Zip Code_____Phone_____

PARTY OR COMPANY SUBJECT TO COMPLAINT

2.   Name_____

Company_____

Address_____

       City_____State_____

Zip   Code_____Phone_____

    Bondsman Involved_____Occurrence date_____

3.   Explain below the facts of your problem or complaint. Also please attach copies of any information you have regarding the matter.

_____

_____

_____

_____
_____
_____
_____
_____
_____
_____
_____
_____
_____
_____

_____

Attach additional sheets if necessary. The affidavit below must be signed
by you, under penalty of perjury, and notarized.

AFFIDAVIT

I, the undersigned, do hereby swear and affirm, under penalty of perjury,
that the facts of my complaint, as well as any evidence and documentation
is support thereof, are true and accurate to the best of my knowledge.

_____   _____
Date   Signature

STATE OF ARKANSAS   )
                                ))SS
COUNTY OF_____   )

     Subscribed and sworn to before me on this_____day of ____, 20___

                                _____
                                Notary Public
MY COMMISSION EXPIRES:

_____

Send this form to: Executive Director
     Professional   Bail Bondsman Licensing Board
     101   East Capitol, Suite 117
     Little   Rock, Arkansas 72201
     Telephone: (501)   682-9050

SAMPLE TELEPHONE LISTING

```
┌─────────────────────────────────────────┐
│                                         │
│        ABC BAIL BOND COMPANY            │
│           1006 Freedom Ave.             │
│             Anytown, AR                 │
│     TOLL FREE # 1/800/222-2222          │
│     Tom Smith, Agent   666-6666         │
│     Fred Brown, Agent  555-5555         │
│                                         │
└─────────────────────────────────────────┘
```

SAMPLE SIGN
OR
BUSINESS CARD

```
┌─────────────────────────────────────────┐
│                                         │
│     ABC BAIL BOND COMPANY               │
│       1006 Freedom Avenue               │
│       Anytown, AR 72222                 │
│                                         │
│                                         │
│     Tom Smith, Agent   666-6666         │
│                                         │
└─────────────────────────────────────────┘
```

APPENDIX "I"

AUTHORIZATION BY SURETY TO ARREST DEFENDANT ON BAIL BOND

TO ALL PERSONS, be it known, that _____(Name of Company)_____, hereinafter referred to as Grantor, does hereby make and grant a limited and specific power of attorney to _____, hereafter referred to as the person designated to apprehend the defendant on bail, and appoint and constitute said individual to act as my attorney-in-fact.

My named attorney-in-fact shall have full power and authority to undertake, commit and perform only the following act(s) on my behalf to the same extent as if I had done so personally, or as I might do, or could do, if personally present, and I am hereby ratifying and confirming all acts said Agent will do or cause to be done by virtue thereof.

The authority granted shall consist of only the following acts:

To locate, apprehend and take into lawful custody the individual(s) known to me as _____ and _____ [who absconded/who may abscond] from the contractual agreement of a lawfully and duly executed bail bond filed by said Grantor with the [District/Circuit] Court of _____ in the [City/Town] of _____ in the County of _____ and in the State of Arkansas whereby said individual's/individuals'] failure to appear [did/will] cause forfeiture of the bail bond posted with said Court by Grantor.

This Limited Power of Attorney shall become null and void after the _____ day of _____, 20___ or by written revocation being properly officiated, with notification of said revocation being received by the person designated to apprehend the defendant on bail via certified mail, return receipt requested.

_____, Grantor
(Corporate Officer, Partner or Sole Proprietor)

STATE OF ARKANSAS   )
)ss
County of _____)

SUBSCRIBED AND SWORN TO before me by _____, known to me, who personally appeared before me this date and signed or acknowledged the foregoing Limited Power of Attorney as his/her free act and deed this _____ day of _____, 19____.

_____
Notary Public

My Commission Expires:

_____

APPENDIX J

Company Name
Address
```
City, State, Zip
```
Phone #

COLLATERAL RECEIPT

- -

Date:_____ 20__   Bond#: <u>XX-____-001000_____</u>

Defendant's Name:_____

Principal's Name:_____

Collateral Received:

_____

_____

_____

_____

_____

_____

    The above-described property is posted as collateral to_____,

for the defendant, named above, until _____.

   No collateral shall be released until the above agreement has been satisfied. If collateral is posted for the security of the bond appearances, no collateral will be released before 31-90 days after confirmation from the clerk of the court that said bond has been exonerated.

<u>Collateral shall be returned to the one who posted it</u>.

    I, the undersigned, do hereby agree to this agreement.

_____   _____
Principal   Bail Bondsman

IF COLLATERAL WAS POSTED FOR SECURITY ON BOND APPEARANCES, OFFICIAL VERIFICATION FROM THE COURT MUST BE PROVIDED TO THIS OFFICE THAT YOUR CASE HAS BEEN COMPLETED BEFORE ANY COLLATERAL IS RELEASED.

RULE AND REGULATION 2
REGULATION OF THE EDUCATION PROGRAM

SECTION

1. Purpose 107
2. Authority 107
3. Effective Date and Applicability 107
4. Definitions 108
5. Application for Course Approval 109
6. Approval or Denial of Course 109
7. Approval of Fee for Continuing Education Course 109
8. Certificate of Completion 110
9. Severability. 110

SECTION 1. PURPOSE

The purpose of this Rule and Regulation ("rule") is to set specific requirements to be followed by the Arkansas Professional Bail Bond Company and Professional Bail Bondsman Licensing Board (Board) in the administration of the beginning and continuing education program, pursuant to Act 909 of 1997, codified as Ark. Code Ann. Sections 17-19-107, and 17-19-402.

SECTION 2. AUTHORITY

This rule is issued pursuant to the authority vested in the Board under Ark. Code Ann. Section 17-19-108 and all other applicable provisions of Arkansas law.

SECTION 3. EFFECTIVE DATE AND APPLICABILITY

This rule shall be effective October 1, 2005 and shall be applicable to the Board and approved beginning and continuing education course providers in the administration of the beginning and continuing education program.

SECTION 4. DEFINITIONS

The following terms as used in this rule shall have the following definitions:

A.   Board – the Arkansas Professional Bail Bond Company and Professional Bail Bondsman Licensing Board/Arkansas Professional Bail Bondsman Licensing Board;

B.   Director – the Executive Director of the Board;

C.   Beginning Education – a course covering Arkansas Code and Regulations related to the bail bond industry and taken prior to licensing.

D.   Continuing Education – post-licensure education derived from participation in courses in bail bond related subjects.

E.   CEC – continuing education credit;

F.   Credit hour – An instructional classroom session of at least fifty (50) minutes with a Board approved instructor present.

G.   Instructor – a person registered and approved by the Board to teach bail bond related subjects.

H.   Licensee – a natural person who is licensed by the Board as a bail bondsman;

I.   Proof of completion – the certificate of attendance awarded by the Board approved instructor.

SECTION 5. APPLICATION FOR COURSE APPROVAL

A. All proposed Beginning and Continuing Education course outlines must be submitted to the Board for review. No course shall be certified until approved by the Board.

B. Approval of courses shall be required annually. Course providers desiring approval for the upcoming year shall submit the proposed course outlines by November 1 to be considered and approved at the December Board meeting.

C. A bail bond company shall be allowed to offer qualifying continuing education courses if the course has been approved by the Board, and the classes are attended by and monitored by a Board approved course provider other than the company course provider who certifies the bail bondsmen have completed six (6) hours of continuing education as approved by the Board. All approved classes must be offered at a neutral location. Classes conducted on the premises of any bail bond company will not be approved. Any continuing education course offered by a bail bond company must be open to attendance by bail bondsmen from other companies at the same cost paid by bail bondsmen from the presenting company.

D. Education providers must notify the Board office, in writing, of the date, time and location of beginning or continuing education classes two (2) weeks prior to the class being offered.

SECTION 6. APPROVAL OR DENIAL OF COURSE

A. Properly completed course outlines will be submitted for consideration by the Board.

B. The Board will review the proposed course outlines. Final approval of course outlines shall be the responsibility of the Board.

SECTION 7. APPROVAL OF FEE FOR BEGINNING AND CONTINUING EDUCATION CLASSES

A. Proposed course outlines shall include a schedule of fees applicable to said classes.

B.   Such schedule of fees shall be subject to the approval of the Board.

SECTION 8.   CERTIFICATE OF COMPLETION

A.   At the completion of each class, an attendance list shall be provided to the Board within two weeks of course completion.

B.   At the completion of each class, students who satisfactorily complete a course shall be awarded a certificate of attendance containing the following information:

> (a) Name of school or sponsor
>
> (b) Name of student (applicant or licensee)
>
> (c) License number – if licensed
>
> (d) Course title
>
> (e) Course location
>
> (f) Course date(s)
>
> (g) Number of classroom hours of instruction
>
> (h) Instructor's signature

SECTION 9.   SEVERABILITY

Any section or provision of this rule held by the court to be invalid or unconstitutional will not affect the validity of any other section or provision.

IRS FORM 8300

REPORTING CASH TRANSACTIONS OVER $10,000

26 U.S.C. § 6050I. 113
    Authors' Endnotes to § 6050I. 116

IRS's Frequently Asked Questions. 119

IRS Form 8300 (http://www.irs.gov/pub/irs-pdf/f8300.pdf)
    www.irs.gov; search for "8300". 126

§ 6050I. Returns relating to cash received in trade or business, etc.

(a) Cash receipts of more than $10,000

Any person—
(1)   who is engaged in a trade or business, and
(2)   who, in the course of such trade or business, receives more than $10,000 in cash in 1 transaction (or 2 or more related transactions),
shall make the return described in subsection (b) with respect to such transaction (or related transactions) at such time as the Secretary may by regulations prescribe.

(b) Form and manner of returns

A return is described in this subsection if such return—
(1)   is in such form as the Secretary may prescribe,[1]
(2)   contains—
    (A)   the name, address, and TIN[2] of the person from whom the cash was received,
    (B)   the amount of cash received,
    (C)   the date and nature of the transaction, and
    (D)   such other information as the Secretary may prescribe.

(c) Exceptions

(1)   Cash received by financial institutions

Subsection (a) shall not apply to—
    (A)   cash received in a transaction reported under title 31, United States Code, if the Secretary determines that reporting under this section would duplicate the reporting to the Treasury under title 31, United States Code, or
    (B)   cash received by any financial institution (as defined in . . . section 5312 (a)(2) of title 31, United States Code).

---

[1] Form 8300 is the prescribed form. It has existed since about 1985.

[2] TIN is tax identification number, and it should be a Social Security number.

(2)   Transactions occurring outside the United States

        Except to the extent provided in regulations prescribed by the Secretary, subsection (a) shall not apply to any transaction if the entire transaction occurs outside the United States.

(d)   Cash includes foreign currency and certain monetary instruments[3]

For purposes of this section, the term "cash" includes—
(1)   foreign currency, and
(2)   to the extent provided in regulations prescribed by the Secretary, any monetary instrument (whether or not in bearer form) with a face amount of not more than $10,000.
Paragraph (2) shall not apply to any check drawn on the account of the writer in a financial institution referred to in subsection (c)(1)(B).

(e)   Statements to be furnished to persons with respect to whom information is required

        Every person required to make a return under subsection (a) shall furnish to each person whose name is required to be set forth in such return a written statement showing—
(1)   the name, address, and phone number of the information contact of the person required to make such return, and
(2)   the aggregate amount of cash described in subsection (a) received by the person required to make such return.
The written statement required under the preceding sentence shall be furnished to the person on or before January 31 of the year following the calendar year for which the return under subsection (a) was required to be made.

---

[3] See FAQ 6:

6.   **What does "cash" mean for the purposes of Form 8300?**
        Cash is money. It is currency and coins of the United States and any other country. Cash is also certain monetary instruments – a cashier's check, bank draft, traveler's check, or money order – if it has a face amount of $10,000 or less and the business receives it in:
        o   A "designated reporting transaction" as defined in Treas. Reg. section 1.6050I-1(c)(iii) (generally, a retail sale of a consumer durable, a collectible, a travel or entertainment activity) or
        o   Any transaction in which the recipient knows the payer is trying to avoid the reporting of the transaction on Form 8300.

(f)   Structuring transactions to evade reporting requirements prohibited

(1)   In general

No person shall for the purpose of evading the return requirements of this section—

    (A)   cause or attempt to cause a trade or business to fail to file a return required under this section,

    (B)   cause or attempt to cause a trade or business to file a return required under this section that contains a material omission or misstatement of fact, or

    (C)   structure or assist in structuring, or attempt to structure or assist in structuring, any transaction with one or more trades or businesses.

(2)   Penalties

A person violating paragraph (1) of this subsection shall be subject to the same civil and criminal sanctions applicable to a person which fails to file or completes a false or incorrect return under this section.[4]

(g)   Cash received by criminal court clerks

(1)   In general

Every clerk of a Federal or State criminal court who receives more than $10,000 in cash as bail for any individual charged with a specified criminal offense shall make a return described in paragraph (2) (at such time as the Secretary may by regulations prescribe) with respect to the receipt of such bail.

(2)   Return

A return is described in this paragraph if such return—

    (A)   is in such form as the Secretary may prescribe, and

    (B)   contains—

        (i)   the name, address, and TIN of—

            (I)   the individual charged with the specified criminal offense, and

            (II)   each person posting the bail (other than a person licensed as a bail bondsman),

        (ii)   the amount of cash received,

        (iii)   the date the cash was received, and

        (iv)   such other information as the Secretary may prescribe.

(3)   Specified criminal offense[5]

For purposes of this subsection, the term "specified criminal offense" means—

---

[4] 26 U.S.C. § 7206 (felony punishable up to three years).

[5] This is a reference to money laundering, a separate crime.

(A)   any Federal criminal offense involving a controlled substance,

(B)   racketeering (as defined in section 1951, 1952, or 1955 of title 18, United States Code),

(C)   money laundering (as defined in section 1956 or 1957 of such title), and

(D)   any State criminal offense substantially similar to an offense described in subparagraph (A), (B), or (C).

(4)   Information to Federal prosecutors

Each clerk required to include on a return under paragraph (1) the information described in paragraph (2)(B) with respect to an individual described in paragraph (2)(B)(i)(I) shall furnish (at such time as the Secretary may by regulations prescribe) a written statement showing such information to the United States Attorney for the jurisdiction in which such individual resides and the jurisdiction in which the specified criminal offense occurred.

(5)   Information to payors of bail

Each clerk required to make a return under paragraph (1) shall furnish (at such time as the Secretary may by regulations prescribe) to each person whose name is required to be set forth in such return by reason of paragraph (2)(B)(i)(II) a written statement showing—

(A)   the name and address of the clerk's office required to make the return, and

(B)   the aggregate amount of cash described in paragraph (1) received by such clerk.

Authors' Endnotes to § 6050I

Failure to file the form:

Willful failure to file the form is a felony, and the funds are subject to forfeiture. 26 U.S.C. § 6050I(f)(2); 26 U.S.C. § 7206 (felony punishable up to three years).

Purpose of the reporting requirement:

Form 8300 Instructions, Page 5, col. 2:

The principal purpose for collecting the information on this form [8300] is to maintain reports or records which have a high degree of usefulness in criminal, tax, or regulatory investigations or proceedings, or in the conduct of intelligence or counterintelligence activities, by directing the federal Government's attention to unusual or questionable transactions.

U.S. v. Butler, 211 F.3d 826 (4th Cir. 2000).

Structuring to avoid reporting is a crime:

Aside from the false form under 26 U.S.C. § 6050I, structuring is a separate felony and leads to forfeiture of the money. 31 U.S.C. § 5313(a), 31 CFR § 103.22(a). *U.S. v. Twenty-Three Thousand Ninety Dollars ($23,090.00) in U.S. Currency,* 377 F. Supp. 2d 1223, 1228 (S.D. Fla. 2005):

> In addition to the required reporting, "[n]o person shall, for the purpose of evading the reporting requirements of section 5316 structure or assist in structuring, or attempt to structure or assist in structuring, any importation or exportation of monetary instruments." 31 U.S.C. § 5324(c)(3). Structuring occurs when an individual alters his transaction in such a way in order to avoid the reporting requirement. *U.S. v. Davenport,* 929 F.2d 1169 (7th Cir. 1991). See also *U.S. v. Ahmad,* 213 F.3d 805, 809 (4th Cir. 2000) (finding that deposits that were structured to avoid the reporting requirement violated 31 U.S.C. § 5324).

Structuring appears to be money laundering the proceeds of crime, a separate felony. 18 U.S.C. §§ 1956, 1957. Am. Jur. 2d *Money* § 67:

> It is a criminal act to structure transactions for the purpose of evading reporting requirements, such as by breaking up a single transaction above the reporting threshold amount into two or more separate transactions. Specific provision is made by statute prohibiting structuring transactions to evade reporting requirements with regard to: domestic coin and currency transactions involving financial institutions; domestic coin and currency transactions involving nonfinancial trades or businesses; and international monetary instrument transactions. The purpose of the antistructuring law is to prevent people from defeating the goal of the requirement that large cash deposits be reported to the Internal Revenue Service.
>
> To convict a defendant of structuring currency transactions to avoid currency reporting requirements, the government is required to prove that:
> (1) the defendant in fact engaged in acts of structuring;
> (2) he or she did so with knowledge that the financial institutions involved were legally obligated to report currency transactions in excess of $10,000; and
> (3) he or she acted with intent to evade that reporting requirement.
>
> To establish that a defendant willfully violated the antistructuring

law, the government must prove that the defendant acted with knowledge that his or her conduct was unlawful, as currency structuring is not inevitably nefarious.

The statute prohibiting the structuring of transactions in such a way as to avoid currency reporting requirements is not unconstitutionally vague. Furthermore, convictions for both money laundering and structuring of financial transactions are not multiplicitous and do not violate double jeopardy. (footnotes omitted)

C.J.S. *United States* § 163:

Under [the] statute, whoever, knowing that the property involved in a financial transaction represents the proceeds of some form of unlawful activity, conducts or attempts to conduct such a financial transaction which in fact involves the proceeds of specified unlawful activity, with the intent to promote the carrying on of specified unlawful activity, is guilty of money laundering.

To convict a defendant of money laundering, the government must prove that he or she knowingly engaged in a financial transaction with the proceeds of unlawful activity, and that he or she knew the transactions involved criminally derived property. While to sustain a conviction the defendant must have known that the primary predicate activity was unlawful, he or she need not have known that the secondary act of laundering the proceeds was unlawful.

"Proceeds" need not consist of money or some tangible asset. The statute does not define "proceeds," but the courts have adopted dictionary definitions that define the term broadly. (footnotes omitted)

Structuring is stupid. Do not do it.
File any required reports.
You have nothing to hide.

IRS FAQs regarding Reporting Cash Payments of Over $10,000 (Form 8300)

http://www.irs.gov/businesses/small/article/0,,id=148821,00.html
Page Last Reviewed or Updated: February 4, 2010

* Filing Requirements
* Written Statement to Customer
* Reportable Transactions

Filing Requirements:

1. **Who must file Form 8300?**
   Any persons who receive more than $10,000 while conducting their trade or business must file a Form 8300. The $10,000 may occur in a single transaction, or a series of related transactions.

2. **What payments must be reported?**
   A business must file Form 8300 to report cash paid to it if the cash payment is:
   o   Over $10,000,
   o   Received as:
      1. One lump sum of over $10,000,
      2. Two or more related payments that total in excess of $10,000, or
      3. Payments received as part of a single transaction (or two or more related transactions) that cause the total cash received within a 12-month period to total more than $10,000.
   o   Received in the course of trade or business,
   o   Received from the same buyer (or agent), and
   o   Received in a single transaction or in two or more related transactions.

3. **What is the definition of a transaction?**
   A transaction is the underlying event resulting in the transfer of cash. Examples include:
   o   Sale of goods, services or real or intangible property
   o   Rental of goods or real or personal property
   o   Cash exchanged for other cash
   o   Establishment, maintenance of or contribution to a trust or escrow account
   o   A loan repayment
   o   Conversion of cash to a negotiable instrument such as a check or a bond

4. **What is a related transaction?**
   Transactions between a buyer, or agent of the buyer, and a seller that occur within a 24-hour period are related transactions.

In addition, transactions more than 24 hours apart are related if the recipient of the cash knows, or has reason to know, that each transaction is one of a series of connected transactions.

5. **Does the 24-hour period mean one day such as all day Tuesday or does it mean literally 24 hours such as from 11:00 am on Tuesday to 11:00 am on Wednesday?**

   A 24-hour period is 24 hours, not necessarily a calendar day or banking day.

6. **What does "cash" mean for the purposes of Form 8300?**

   Cash is money. It is currency and coins of the United States and any other country. Cash is also certain monetary instruments – a cashier's check, bank draft, traveler's check, or money order – if it has a face amount of $10,000 or less and the business receives it in:

   o   A "designated reporting transaction" as defined in Treas. Reg. section 1.6050I-1(c)(iii) (generally, a retail sale of a consumer durable, a collectible, a travel or entertainment activity) or

   o   Any transaction in which the recipient knows the payer is trying to avoid the reporting of the transaction on Form 8300.

7. **What is a designated reporting transaction?**

   Generally, a designated reporting transaction is the retail sale of any of the following:

   o   A consumer durable, such as an automobile or boat. Property is generally a consumer durable if it is tangible personal property (not real or intangible property) that:

   - Is generally suited for personal use,
   - Is expected to last at least one year under ordinary use, and
   - Has a sale price of more than $10,000.

   o   A collectible (such as a work of art, rug, antique, metal, gem, stamp, or coin)

   o   An item of travel and entertainment (if the total sales price of all items for the same trip or entertainment event is more than $10,000).

8. **If an item (e.g. automobile) sells for $9,950 but the buyer pays $10,650 (sales price plus state and local taxes), would this be considered a designated reporting transaction (retail sale of a consumer durable) requiring the definition of cash to be expanded to include monetary instruments?**

   In determining a designated reporting transaction, a consumer durable is defined as tangible personal property that is generally suited for personal use, is expected to last at least one year under ordinary use, and has a sale price of more than $10,000 (exclusive of sales tax). If the sales price is less than $10,000, then the tangible personal property would not be a consumer durable regardless of any taxes.

9. **Does a wholesaler report transactions paid in US (or foreign) coins and currency only?**
Yes, if the wholesaler receives payment in the form of coins or currency. A wholesaler, however, need not report transactions paid with cashier's checks, bank drafts, traveler's checks, or money orders.

10. **What if a retailer also does some wholesale transactions, must the business report all transactions, or just the retail ones?**
If the trade or business of the seller principally consists of sales to ultimate consumers, the all sales, including wholesale transactions, are considered "retail sales" and are subject to the Form 8300 reporting requirements.

11. **Is a personal check considered cash for reporting on Form 8300?**
Personal checks are not considered cash.

12. **Would a Mobile Home be classified as personal or real property for purposes of filing Form 8300?**
A retail sale of a mobile home is personal property. A mobile home qualifies as personal property and a consumable durable for determining any required Form 8300 reporting, regardless of how the purchaser intends to use or ultimately uses the mobile home.

13. **When is the Form 8300 due?**
A business must file Form 8300 within 15 days after the date the cash was received. If there are subsequent payments that are made with respect to a single transaction (or two or more related transactions), the business should file the form 8300 when the total amount paid exceeds $10,000. Each time the payments aggregate in excess of $10,000 the business must file another form 8300 within 15 days of the payment that causes the additional payments to total more than $10,000.

14. **If the business is unable to obtain the Taxpayer Identification Number of a customer making a cash payment of over ten thousand dollars, should the business file Form 8300 anyway?**
Yes, the business should file Form 8300 with a statement explaining why the Taxpayer Identification Number is not included.

15. **How can a business get Form 8300?**
Form 8300 is available in English or Spanish:
o   Via the telephone on the IRS forms line at 1-800-829-3676
o   Via the internet at the IRS.gov website or FinCEN website.

16. **Are there any publications that will help with filing Form 8300?**
Yes. Publication 1544, Reporting Cash Payments of Over $10,000 (Received in a

Trade or Business) explains why, when, and where to file Form 8300. It also explains key issues and terms related to Form 8300. This publication is available in English or Spanish:

o   At the IRS forms line at 1-800-829-3676 or
o   On the internet at the IRS.gov website.

17.   **Where does a business file Form 8300?**
A business should mail Form 8300 to:

> Internal Revenue Service
> Detroit Computing Center
> P.O. Box 32621
> Detroit, MI 48232

18.   **How can a filer confirm that a filed Form 8300 has been received by IRS?**
The filer can confirm the IRS received the Form 8300 by:

o   Sending the form via certified mail with return receipt requested or
o   Calling the Detroit Computing Center at 1-800-800-2877.
If a customer (the buyer) about whom the Form 8300 was filed wants a copy of the form, they must contact the filer.

19.   **Does the IRS have an email address to send questions regarding Form 8300?**
You can send questions concerning Form 8300 to 8300QUESTIONS@IRS.GOV. The email system will not accept actual Forms 8300.

Written Statement to Customer:

1.   **Must a business notify its customer that the business has filed a Form 8300 regarding the cash transaction with the customer?**
Yes, a business must notify its customer, in writing, by January 31 of the subsequent calendar year.

2.   **If a business filed a Form 8300 on an individual and checked the suspicious transaction box and an 8300 report was not required, does the business have to inform the individual by January 30 about the fact that it filed Form 8300?**
No, because reporting of the suspicious transaction in this instance is voluntary. A business is only required to provide a statement to individuals if the filing of the Form 8300 is required. A business is prohibited from informing the buyer that the suspicious transaction box was checked.

3.   **Instead of sending the customer a separate notification letter, can the dealership use the sales invoice as the notification requirement, if the sales invoice has language printed on it that the IRS will be furnished with**

information for cash sales over $10,000?

There is nothing in the code or regulations mandating a specific format for the customer statement. The regulations, however, establish certain minimum requirements. As long as these minimum requirements are met, there would be no problem if the seller chose to print the required language on an invoice. Treasury Regulation section 1.6050I-1(f)(2) states:

- ○ Form of statement. The statement required by the preceding paragraph need not follow any particular format, but it must contain the following information:
  - ■ The name and address of the person making the return;
  - ■ The aggregate amount of reportable cash, received by the person who filed the Form 8300 during the calendar year, in all related cash transactions; and
  - ■ A legend stating that the information contained in the statement is being reported to the Internal Revenue Service.

4.   **Can a copy of the Form 8300 be given to the customer as a written notice?**

Yes, since the Form 8300 contains the name, address, contact telephone number of the filer, aggregate amount of reportable cash received and informs the notice that the payment(s) are being reported to the IRS, the Form 8300 would be acceptable as written notification. However, if during the calendar year, the filer has transactions with the notice which were included on more than one Form 8300, furnishing copies to the notice of multiple Forms 8300 does not meet the notice requirement because it is not a "single" statement. In this situation, the Form 8300 filer should provide a single written notice for all of the transactions. It should be noted that while the practice of using a copy of the Form 8300 as a notice may be convenient, it may not be advisable because of the sensitive information contained on the form; e.g. Employer Identification Number (EIN) or Social Security Number (SSN).

Reportable Transactions:

. . .

3.   **A customer purchased a vehicle several months ago for $9,000 cash. Within the next 12 months, the customer paid the dealership additional cash of $1,500 for items relating to the vehicle such as a repair to the vehicle's transmission, purchase of accessories and a customized paint job, etc. Is the dealership required to file a Form 8300 for these transactions?**

No, unless the dealer knew or had reason to know the sale of the vehicle and the subsequent transactions were a series of connected transactions (for example, if the dealer and the customer agreed, as a condition of the sale of the vehicle, that the customer would be obligated to pay the additional $1,500).

4. **A customer wired $7,000 from his bank account to the dealership's bank account and also presented a $4,000 cashier check. Does the dealership complete Form 8300?**

    A wire transfer does not constitute cash for Form 8300 reporting. Since the remaining cash remitted was below $10,000, the dealer has no filing requirement.

5. **A taxi driver makes weekly payments in cash to a taxi company as a lease payment. During a twelve-month period, these payments total more than $10,000. Are these payments considered related transactions and is the taxi company required to file a Form 8300?**

    Yes, the weekly lease payments constitute payments on the same transaction (the leasing of the cab). Accordingly, the taxi company is required to file Form 8300 when the total amount exceeds $10,000. Each time the payments aggregate in excess of $10,000 the taxi company must file another form 8300 within 15 days of the payment that causes the additional payments to total more than $10,000.

6. **A husband and wife purchase two cars at one time from the same dealer and the total cash received $10,200. How many Form 8300s should the car dealer file?**

    The transaction can be viewed as either a single transaction or two related transactions. Either way, it warrants only one Form 8300.

7. **Regarding related transactions, if a customer purchased an item, then eight weeks later the same customer purchased a different item, are these amounts aggregated and reported on the Form 8300?**

    No, if the two payments are for separate unrelated transactions.

8. **If a person gives a bail bonding agent more than 10k cash in anticipation of being arrested but has not been arrested yet, is the bail bondsman required to report the cash received, although no service has been performed at the time the cash is received?**

    Yes, once a person (whether bail bond agent, attorney, or other) receives (in a transaction or related transactions) cash exceeding $10,000 in the person's trade or business (bail bonds, legal services, etc.) a Form 8300 must be filed.

9. **Health services entities often have transactions that will engender over $10,000 in fees in one visit (i.e. an ER visit). Uninsured patients often pay via installment payments and may use cashiers checks, etc., that are less than $10,000 individually. Would this type of transaction be reportable?**

    When an installment arrangement is established on a single transaction, in this case the providing of emergency room services, the hospital must file a Form 8300 when cash payments received exceed $10,000 within a 12-month period. After filing the Form 8300, a new count of cash payments from the patient would begin. Since this is not a "designated reporting transaction," you would not expand the definition of cash to include monetary instruments, like cashiers checks, unless you know that the payer is trying by the manner of payment to keep you from reporting on Form 8300 the transaction or payment(s).

. . .

11. **A customer deposited over $10,000 in cash into his bank account, which was obtained from a sale of heavy equipment. Is there a form the bank has to file?**
The law requires the financial institution that receives a deposit of more than $10,000 to submit a Currency Transaction Report (CTR) to the Treasury. The fact that this was a result of a sale of heavy equipment has no bearing.

12. **If a customer purchased a cashier's check at the bank for over $10,000, would the bank report the transaction? Does the seller of a vehicle need to report the transaction if the same cashier's check is subsequently used to purchase a vehicle?**
The bank is required to file a Currency Transaction Report (not a Form 8300) in this scenario. Generally, the purchase of a vehicle with a cashier's check that is over $10,000 should not be reported on Form 8300. A cashier's check, bank draft, traveler's check, or money order with a face amount of more than $10,000 is not treated as cash and a business does not have to file Form 8300 when it receives them. These items are not defined as cash because, if they were bought with currency, the bank or other financial institution that issued them must file a Currency Transaction Report (CTR).

Report of Cash Payments Over $10,000
Received in a Trade or Business

▶ See instructions for definition of cash.

▶ Use this form for transactions occurring after March 31, 2008. Do not use prior versions after this date.

For Privacy Act and Paperwork Reduction Act Notice, see page 5.

FinCEN Form **8300**

(Rev. March 2008)
OMB No. 1506-0018

Department of the Treasury
Financial Crimes
Enforcement Network

1 Check appropriate box(es) if: **a** ☐ Amends prior report;   **b** ☐ Suspicious transaction.

Part I   Identity of Individual From Whom the Cash Was Received

2 If more than one individual is involved, check here and see instructions . . . . ▶ ☐

3 Last name	**4** First name	**5** M.I.	**6** Taxpayer identification number

7 Address (number, street, and apt. or suite no.)	**8** Date of birth . ▶ M M D D Y Y Y Y (see instructions)

9 City	**10** State	**11** ZIP code	**12** Country (if not U.S.)	**13** Occupation, profession, or business

14 Identifying document (ID)   **a** Describe ID ▶ ....   **b** Issued by ▶ ....
   c Number ▶

Part II   Person on Whose Behalf This Transaction Was Conducted

15 If this transaction was conducted on behalf of more than one person, check here and see instructions . . . . . . ▶ ☐

16 Individual's last name or Organization's name	**17** First name	**18** M.I.	**19** Taxpayer identification number

20 Doing business as (DBA) name (see instructions)	Employer identification number

21 Address (number, street, and apt. or suite no.)	**22** Occupation, profession, or business

23 City	**24** State	**25** ZIP code	**26** Country (if not U.S.)

27 Alien identification (ID)   **a** Describe ID ▶ ....   **b** Issued by ▶ ....
   c Number ▶

Part III   Description of Transaction and Method of Payment

28 Date cash received M M D D Y Y Y Y	**29** Total cash received $ .00	**30** If cash was received in more than one payment, check here . . . . ▶ ☐	**31** Total price if different from item 29 $ .00

32 Amount of cash received (in U.S. dollar equivalent) (must equal item 29) (see instructions):

   a U.S. currency $ _____ .00   (Amount in $100 bills or higher $ _____ .00)

   b Foreign currency $ _____ .00   (Country ▶ _____)

   c Cashier's check(s) $ _____ .00   Issuer's name(s) and serial number(s) of the monetary instrument(s) ▶

   d Money order(s) $ _____ .00

   e Bank draft(s) $ _____ .00

   f Traveler's check(s) $ _____ .00

33 Type of transaction

   a ☐ Personal property purchased   **f** ☐ Debt obligations paid
   b ☐ Real property purchased   **g** ☐ Exchange of cash
   c ☐ Personal services provided   **h** ☐ Escrow or trust funds
   d ☐ Business services provided   **i** ☐ Bail received by court clerks
   e ☐ Intangible property purchased   **j** ☐ Other (specify in item 34) ▶

34 Specific description of property or service shown in 33. Give serial or registration number, address, docket number, etc. ▶ ....
....
....

Part IV   Business That Received Cash

35 Name of business that received cash	**36** Employer identification number

37 Address (number, street, and apt. or suite no.)	Social security number

38 City	**39** State	**40** ZIP code	**41** Nature of your business

42 Under penalties of perjury, I declare that to the best of my knowledge the information I have furnished above is true, correct, and complete.

Signature ▶ _____   Title ▶ _____
       Authorized official

43 Date of signature M M D D Y Y Y Y	**44** Type or print name of contact person	**45** Contact telephone number ( )

Multiple Parties
(Complete applicable parts below if box 2 or 15 on page 1 is checked)

Part I Continued—Complete if box 2 on page 1 is checked

3 Last name	4 First name	5 M.I.	6 Taxpayer identification number

7 Address (number, street, and apt. or suite no.)	8 Date of birth . . ▶ (see instructions)	M M D D Y Y Y Y

9 City	10 State	11 ZIP code	12 Country (if not U.S.)	13 Occupation, profession, or business

14 Identifying document (ID)	a Describe ID ▶	b Issued by ▶ ....
	c Number ▶	

3 Last name	4 First name	5 M.I.	6 Taxpayer identification number

7 Address (number, street, and apt. or suite no.)	8 Date of birth . . ▶ (see instructions)	M M D D Y Y Y Y

9 City	10 State	11 ZIP code	12 Country (if not U.S.)	13 Occupation, profession, or business

14 Identifying document (ID)	a Describe ID ▶	b Issued by ▶ ....
	c Number ▶	

Part II Continued—Complete if box 15 on page 1 is checked

16 Individual's last name or Organization's name	17 First name	18 M.I.	19 Taxpayer identification number

20 Doing business as (DBA) name (see instructions)	Employer identification number

21 Address (number, street, and apt. or suite no.)	22 Occupation, profession, or business

23 City	24 State	25 ZIP code	26 Country (if not U.S.)

27 Alien identification (ID)	a Describe ID ▶	b Issued by ▶ ....
	c Number ▶	

16 Individual's last name or Organization's name	17 First name	18 M.I.	19 Taxpayer identification number

20 Doing business as (DBA) name (see instructions)	Employer identification number

21 Address (number, street, and apt. or suite no.)	22 Occupation, profession, or business

23 City	24 State	25 ZIP code	26 Country (if not U.S.)

27 Alien identification (ID)	a Describe ID ▶	b Issued by ▶ ....
	c Number ▶	

Comments – Please use the lines provided below to comment on or clarify any information you entered on any line in Parts I, II, III, and IV

_____

_____

_____

_____

Section references are to the Internal Revenue Code unless otherwise noted.

Important Reminders

● Section 6050I (26 United States Code (U.S.C.) 6050I) and 31 U.S.C. 5331 require that certain information be reported to the IRS and the Financial Crimes Enforcement Network (FinCEN). This information must be reported on IRS/FinCEN Form 8300.

● Item 33 box i is to be checked only by clerks of the court; box d is to be checked by bail bondsmen. See the instructions on page 5.

● The meaning of the word "currency" for purposes of 31 U.S.C. 5331 is the same as for the word "cash" (See *Cash* on page 4).

General Instructions

Who must file. Each person engaged in a trade or business who, in the course of that trade or business, receives more than $10,000 in cash in one transaction or in two or more related transactions, must file Form 8300. Any transactions conducted between a payer (or its agent) and the recipient in a 24-hour period are related transactions. Transactions are considered related even if they occur over a period of more than 24 hours if the recipient knows, or has reason to know, that each transaction is one of a series of connected transactions.

Keep a copy of each Form 8300 for 5 years from the date you file it.

Clerks of federal or state courts must file Form 8300 if more than $10,000 in cash is received as bail for an individual(s) charged with certain criminal offenses. For these purposes, a clerk includes the clerk's office or any other office, department, division, branch, or unit of the court that is authorized to receive bail. If a person receives bail on behalf of a clerk, the clerk is treated as receiving the bail. See the instructions for Item 33 on page 5.

If multiple payments are made in cash to satisfy bail and the initial payment does not exceed $10,000, the initial payment and subsequent payments must be aggregated and the information return must be filed by the 15th day after receipt of the payment that causes the aggregate amount to exceed $10,000 in cash. In such cases, the reporting requirement can be satisfied either by sending a single written statement with an aggregate amount listed or by furnishing a copy of each Form 8300 relating to that payer. Payments made to satisfy separate bail requirements are not required to be aggregated. See Treasury Regulations section 1.6050I-2.

Casinos must file Form 8300 for nongaming activities (restaurants, shops, etc.).

Voluntary use of Form 8300. Form 8300 may be filed voluntarily for any suspicious transaction (see *Definitions* on page 4) for use by FinCEN and the IRS, even if the total amount does not exceed $10,000.

Exceptions. Cash is not required to be reported if it is received:

● By a financial institution required to file Form 104, Currency Transaction Report.

● By a casino required to file (or exempt from filing) Form 103, Currency Transaction Report by Casinos, if the cash is received as part of its gaming business.

● By an agent who receives the cash from a principal, if the agent uses all of the cash within 15 days in a second transaction that is reportable on Form 8300 or on Form 104, and discloses all the information necessary to complete Part II of Form 8300 or Form 104 to the recipient of the cash in the second transaction.

● In a transaction occurring entirely outside the United States. See Publication 1544, Reporting Cash Payments of Over $10,000 (Received in a Trade or Business), regarding transactions occurring in Puerto Rico and territories and possessions of the United States.

● In a transaction that is not in the course of a person's trade or business.

When to file. File Form 8300 by the 15th day after the date the cash was received. If that date falls on a Saturday, Sunday, or legal holiday, file the form on the next business day.

Where to file. File the form with the Internal Revenue Service, Detroit Computing Center, P.O. Box 32621, Detroit, MI 48232.

Statement to be provided. You must give a written or electronic statement to each person named on a required Form 8300 on or before January 31 of the year following the calendar year in which the cash is received. The statement must show the name, telephone number, and address of the information contact for the business, the aggregate amount of reportable cash received, and that the information was furnished to the IRS. Keep a copy of the statement for your records.

Multiple payments. If you receive more than one cash payment for a single transaction or for related transactions, you must report the multiple payments any time you receive a total amount that exceeds $10,000 within any 12-month period. Submit the report within 15 days of the date you receive the payment that

causes the total amount to exceed $10,000. If more than one report is required within 15 days, you may file a combined report. File the combined report no later than the date the earliest report, if filed separately, would have to be filed.

Taxpayer identification number (TIN). You must furnish the correct TIN of the person or persons from whom you receive the cash and, if applicable, the person or persons on whose behalf the transaction is being conducted. You may be subject to penalties for an incorrect or missing TIN.

The TIN for an individual (including a sole proprietorship) is the individual's social security number (SSN). For certain resident aliens who are not eligible to get an SSN and nonresident aliens who are required to file tax returns, it is an IRS Individual Taxpayer Identification Number (ITIN). For other persons, including corporations, partnerships, and estates, it is the employer identification number (EIN).

If you have requested but are not able to get a TIN for one or more of the parties to a transaction within 15 days following the transaction, file the report and attach a statement explaining why the TIN is not included.

Exception: *You are not required to provide the TIN of a person who is a nonresident alien individual or a foreign organization if that person or foreign organization:*

● *Does not have income effectively connected with the conduct of a U.S. trade or business;*

● *Does not have an office or place of business, or a fiscal or paying agent in the United States;*

● *Does not furnish a withholding certificate described in §1.1441-1(e)(2) or (3) or §1.1441-5(c)(2)(iv) or (3)(iii) to the extent required under §1.1441-1(e)(4)(vii); or*

● *Does not have to furnish a TIN on any return, statement, or other document as required by the income tax regulations under section 897 or 1445.*

Penalties. You may be subject to penalties if you fail to file a correct and complete Form 8300 on time and you cannot show that the failure was due to reasonable cause. You may also be subject to penalties if you fail to furnish timely a correct and complete statement to each person named in a required report. A minimum penalty of $25,000 may be imposed if the failure is due to an intentional or willful disregard of the cash reporting requirements.

Penalties may also be imposed for causing, or attempting to cause, a trade or business to fail to file a required report; for causing, or attempting to cause, a trade or business to file a required report containing a material omission or misstatement of fact; or for structuring, or attempting to structure, transactions to avoid the reporting requirements. These violations may also be subject to criminal prosecution which, upon conviction, may result in imprisonment of up to 5 years or fines of up to $250,000 for individuals and $500,000 for corporations or both.

Definitions

Cash. The term "cash" means the following:

● U.S. and foreign coin and currency received in any transaction.

● A cashier's check, money order, bank draft, or traveler's check having a face amount of $10,000 or less that is received in a designated reporting transaction (defined below), or that is received in any transaction in which the recipient knows that the instrument is being used in an attempt to avoid the reporting of the transaction under either section 6050I or 31 U.S.C. 5331.

Note. Cash does not include a check drawn on the payer's own account, such as a personal check, regardless of the amount.

Designated reporting transaction. A retail sale (or the receipt of funds by a broker or other intermediary in connection with a retail sale) of a consumer durable, a collectible, or a travel or entertainment activity.

Retail sale. Any sale (whether or not the sale is for resale or for any other purpose) made in the course of a trade or business if that trade or business principally consists of making sales to ultimate consumers.

Consumer durable. An item of tangible personal property of a type that, under ordinary usage, can reasonably be expected to remain useful for at least 1 year, and that has a sales price of more than $10,000.

Collectible. Any work of art, rug, antique, metal, gem, stamp, coin, etc.

Travel or entertainment activity. An item of travel or entertainment that pertains to a single trip or event if the combined sales price of the item and all other items relating to the same trip or event that are sold in the same transaction (or related transactions) exceeds $10,000.

Exceptions. A cashier's check, money order, bank draft, or traveler's check is not considered received in a designated reporting transaction if it constitutes the proceeds of a bank loan or if it is received as a payment on certain promissory notes, installment sales contracts, or down payment plans. See Publication 1544 for more information.

Person. An individual, corporation, partnership, trust, estate, association, or company.

Recipient. The person receiving the cash. Each branch or other unit of a person's trade or business is considered a separate recipient unless the branch receiving the cash (or a central office linking the branches), knows or has reason to know the identity of payers making cash payments to other branches.

Transaction. Includes the purchase of property or services, the payment of debt, the exchange of a negotiable instrument for cash, and the receipt of cash to be held in escrow or trust. A single transaction may not be broken into multiple transactions to avoid reporting.

Suspicious transaction. A suspicious transaction is a transaction in which it appears that a person is attempting to cause Form 8300 not to be filed, or to file a false or incomplete form.

Specific Instructions

You must complete all parts. However, you may skip Part II if the individual named in Part I is conducting the transaction on his or her behalf only. For voluntary reporting of suspicious transactions, see Item 1 below.

Item 1. If you are amending a prior report, check box 1a. Complete the appropriate items with the correct or amended information only. Complete all of Part IV. Staple a copy of the original report to the amended report.

To voluntarily report a suspicious transaction (see *Suspicious transaction* above), check box 1b. You may also telephone your local IRS Criminal Investigation Division or call 1-866-556-3974.

Part I

Item 2. If two or more individuals conducted the transaction you are reporting, check the box and complete Part I for any one of the individuals. Provide the same information for the other individual(s) on the back of the form. If more than three individuals are involved, provide the same information on additional sheets of paper and attach them to this form.

Item 6. Enter the taxpayer identification number (TIN) of the individual named. See *Taxpayer identification number (TIN)* on page 3 for more information.

Item 8. Enter eight numerals for the date of birth of the individual named. For example, if the individual's birth date is July 6, 1960, enter 07 06 1960.

Item 13. Fully describe the nature of the occupation, profession, or business (for example, "plumber," "attorney," or "automobile dealer"). Do not use general or nondescriptive terms such as "businessman" or "self-employed."

Item 14. You must verify the name and address of the named individual(s). Verification must be made by examination of a document normally accepted as a means of identification when cashing checks (for example, a driver's license, passport, alien registration card, or other official document). In item 14a, enter the type of document examined. In item 14b, identify the issuer of the document. In item 14c, enter the document's number. For example, if the individual has a Utah driver's license, enter "driver's license" in item 14a, "Utah" in item 14b, and the number appearing on the license in item 14c.

Note. You must complete all three items (a, b, and c) in this line to make sure that Form 8300 will be processed correctly.

Part II

Item 15. If the transaction is being conducted on behalf of more than one person (including husband and wife or parent and child), check the box and complete Part II for any one of the persons. Provide the same information for the other person(s) on the back of the form. If more than three persons are involved, provide the same information on additional sheets of paper and attach them to this form.

Items 16 through 19. If the person on whose behalf the transaction is being conducted is an individual, complete items 16, 17, and 18. Enter his or her TIN in item 19. If the individual is a sole proprietor and has an employer identification number (EIN), you must enter both the SSN and EIN in item 19. If the person is an organization, put its name as shown on required tax filings in item 16 and its EIN in item 19.

Item 20. If a sole proprietor or organization named in items 16 through 18 is doing business under a name other than that entered in item 16 (for example, a "trade" or "doing business as (DBA)" name), enter it here.

Item 27. If the person is not required to furnish a TIN, complete this item. See *Taxpayer Identification Number (TIN)* on page 3. Enter a description of the type of official document issued to that person in item 27a (for example, a "passport"), the country that issued the document in item 27b, and the document's number in item 27c.

Note. You must complete all three items (a, b, and c) in this line to make sure that Form 8300 will be processed correctly.

Part III

Item 28. Enter the date you received the cash. If you received the cash in more than one payment, enter the date you received the payment that caused the combined amount to exceed $10,000. See *Multiple payments* on page 3 for more information.

Item 30. Check this box if the amount shown in item 29 was received in more than one payment (for example, as installment payments or payments on related transactions).

Item 31. Enter the total price of the property, services, amount of cash exchanged, etc. (for example, the total cost of a vehicle purchased, cost of catering service, exchange of currency) if different from the amount shown in item 29.

Item 32. Enter the dollar amount of each form of cash received. Show foreign currency amounts in U.S. dollar equivalent at a fair market rate of exchange available to the public. The sum of the amounts must equal item 29. For cashier's check, money order, bank draft, or traveler's check, provide the name of the issuer and the serial number of each instrument. Names of all issuers and all serial numbers involved must be provided. If necessary, provide this information on additional sheets of paper and attach them to this form.

Item 33. Check the appropriate box(es) that describe the transaction. If the transaction is not specified in boxes a–i, check box j and briefly describe the transaction (for example, "car lease," "boat lease," "house lease," or "aircraft rental"). If the transaction relates to the receipt of bail by a court clerk, check box i, "Bail received by court clerks." This box is only for use by court clerks. If the transaction relates to cash received by a bail bondsman, check box d, "Business services provided."

Part IV

Item 36. If you are a sole proprietorship, you must enter your SSN. If your business also has an EIN, you must provide the EIN as well. All other business entities must enter an EIN.

Item 41. Fully describe the nature of your business, for example, "attorney" or "jewelry dealer." Do not use general or nondescriptive terms such as "business" or "store."

Item 42. This form must be signed by an individual who has been authorized to do so for the business that received the cash.

Comments

Use this section to comment on or clarify anything you may have entered on any line in Parts I, II, III, and IV. For example, if you checked box b (Suspicious transaction) in line 1 above Part I, you may want to explain why you think that the cash transaction you are reporting on Form 8300 may be suspicious.

Privacy Act and Paperwork Reduction Act Notice. Except as otherwise noted, the information solicited on this form is required by the Internal Revenue Service (IRS) and the Financial Crimes Enforcement Network (FinCEN) in order to carry out the laws and regulations of the United States Department of the Treasury. Trades or businesses, except for clerks of criminal courts, are required to provide the information to the IRS and FinCEN under both section 6050I and 31 U.S.C. 5331. Clerks of criminal courts are required to provide the information to the IRS under section 6050I. Section 6109 and 31 U.S.C. 5331 require that you provide your social security number in order to adequately identify you and process your return and other papers. The principal purpose for collecting the information on this form is to maintain reports or records which have a high degree of usefulness in criminal, tax, or regulatory investigations or proceedings, or in the conduct of intelligence or counterintelligence activities, by directing the federal Government's attention to unusual or questionable transactions.

You are not required to provide information as to whether the reported transaction is deemed suspicious. Failure to provide all other requested information, or providing fraudulent information, may result in criminal prosecution and other penalties under Title 26 and Title 31 of the United States Code.

Generally, tax returns and return information are confidential, as stated in section 6103. However, section 6103 allows or requires the IRS to disclose or give the information requested on this form to others as described in the Code. For example, we may disclose your tax information to the Department of Justice, to enforce the tax laws, both civil and criminal, and to cities, states, the District of Columbia, to carry out their tax laws. We may disclose this information to other persons as necessary to obtain information which we cannot get in any other way. We may disclose this information to federal, state, and local child support agencies; and to other federal agencies for the purposes of determining entitlement for benefits or the eligibility for and the repayment of loans. We may also provide the records to appropriate state, local, and foreign criminal law enforcement and regulatory personnel in the performance of their official duties. We may also disclose this information to other countries under a tax treaty, or to federal and state agencies to enforce federal nontax criminal laws and to combat terrorism. In addition, FinCEN may provide the information to those officials if they are conducting intelligence or counter-intelligence activities to protect against international terrorism.

You are not required to provide the information requested on a form that is subject to the Paperwork Reduction Act unless the form displays a valid OMB control number. Books or records relating to a form or its instructions must be retained as long as their contents may become material in the administration of any law under Title 26 or Title 31.

The time needed to complete this form will vary depending on individual circumstances. The estimated average time is 21 minutes. If you have comments concerning the accuracy of this time estimate or suggestions for making this form simpler, you can write to the Internal Revenue Service, Tax Products Coordinating Committee, SE:W:CAR:MP:T:T:SP, 1111 Constitution Ave. NW, IR-6526, Washington, DC 20224. Do not send Form 8300 to this address. Instead, see *Where to File* on page 3.